THE MAGIC CIRCLE

MAGIC CIRCLE

STORIES AND PEOPLE IN POETRY

EDITED BY LOUIS UNTERMEYER

Illustrated by Beth and Joe Krush

HARCOURT, BRACE AND COMPANY, NEW YORK

ACKNOWLEDGMENTS

BRANDT & BRANDT: "The Ballad of the Harp-Weaver" from *The Harp-Weaver and Other Poems*, published by Harper & Brothers. Copyright, 1920, 1921, 1922, 1923, by Edna St. Vincent Millay. "Nightmare Number Three" from *Selected Works of Stephen Vincent Benét*, published by Rinehart & Company, Inc. Copyright, 1935, by Stephen Vincent Benét; "George Washington" from *A Book of Americans*, published by Rinehart & Company, Inc. Copyright, 1933, by Rosemary and Stephen Vincent Benét.

COWARD-MCCANN, INC.: "The Lady" from *The Creaking Stair* by Elizabeth Coatsworth. Copyright, 1923, by Elizabeth Coatsworth, and 1929, 1949, by Coward-McCann, Inc. Reprinted by permission.

DODD, MEAD & COMPANY: "The Shooting of Dan McGrew" and "The Cremation of Sam McGee" by Robert W. Service. Reprinted by permission of Dodd, Mead & Company from *The Complete Poems of Robert W. Service*. Copyright, 1907, 1909, 1912, by Dodd, Mead & Company. "The Soldier" by Rupert Brooke. Reprinted by permission of Dodd, Mead & Company from *The Collected Poems of Rupert Brooke*. Copyright, 1915, by Dodd, Mead & Company.

E. P. DUTTON & COMPANY, INC.: "Daniel Boone." Taken from *I Sing the Pioneer* by Arthur Guiterman. Published and copyright, 1926, by E. P. Dutton & Company, Inc., New York.

HARPER & BROTHERS: "Old Christmas" from *Lonesome Water* by Roy Helton. Copyright, 1930, by Harper & Brothers.

HENRY HOLT AND COMPANY, INC.: "The Code" and "The Death of the Hired Man" from *Complete Poems of Robert Frost*. Copyright, 1930, 1949, by Henry Holt and Company, Inc. Used by permission of the publishers. "The Listeners" from *Collected Poems* by Walter de la Mare. Copyright, 1920, by Henry Holt and Company, Inc. Copyright, 1948, by Walter de la Mare. Used by permission of the publishers.

ALFRED A. KNOPF, INC.: "Jim." Reprinted from *Cautionary Verses* by Hilaire Belloc, by permission of Alfred A. Knopf, Inc. Copyright, 1931, by Hilaire Belloc. "Peter and John." Reprinted from *The Collected Poems of Elinor Wylie*, by Elinor Wylie, copyright, 1928, 1932, by Alfred A. Knopf, Inc. "Dunkirk." From *Dunkirk* by Robert Nathan, copyright, 1941, by Robert Nathan. Reprinted by permission of Alfred A. Knopf, Inc.

J. B. LIPPINCOTT COMPANY: "The Highwayman" by Alfred Noyes, from *Collected Poems in One Volume by Alfred Noyes.* Copyright, 1906, 1934, and 1947, by J. B. Lippincott Company.

LITTLE, BROWN & COMPANY: "The Boy Who Laughed At Santa Claus" from *Good Intentions.* Copyright, 1942, by Ogden Nash. Reprinted by permission of Little, Brown & Company.

ESTATE OF E. L. MASTERS: "Achilles Deatheridge" from *The Great Valley* by Edgar Lee Masters. Published by The Macmillan Company; copyright 1917. Reprinted by special permission of Ellen C. Masters.

MCINTOSH AND OTIS, INC.: "Andrew Jackson" from *Brady's Bend* by Martha Keller. Copyright, 1946, by Martha Keller Rowland, and published by Rutgers University Press.

RANDOM HOUSE, INC.: "Ballad" (XXIV of "Songs and Other Musical Pieces") from *The Collected Poetry of W. H. Auden.* Reprinted by permission of Random House, Inc. Copyright, 1945, by W. H. Auden.

THE SATURDAY REVIEW OF LITERATURE: "How We Logged Katahdin Stream" by Daniel G. Hoffman. Reprinted by permission of the author and *The Saturday Review of Literature.*

CHARLES SCRIBNER'S SONS: "Miniver Cheevy" from *The Town Down the River* by Edwin Arlington Robinson. Reprinted from *The Town Down the River* by Edwin Arlington Robinson. Copyright, 1910, by Charles Scribner's Sons, 1938, by Ruth Nivison; used by permission of the publishers.

SHAPIRO, BERNSTEIN & CO. INC.: "Casey Jones," words by T. Lawrence Seibert, music by Eddie Newton. Copyright, 1909, by Newton and Seibert. Copyright renewed, assigned to Shapiro, Bernstein & Co. Inc.

THE VIKING PRESS, INC.: "Story" by Dorothy Parker from *The Portable Dorothy Parker.* Copyright, 1928, 1944, by Dorothy Parker. Reprinted by permission of The Viking Press, Inc., New York.

The poems by Michael Lewis, Joseph Lauren, Daniel G. Hoffman, and Carolyn Wells are reprinted by special permission of the authors. The translations and adaptations by Louis Untermeyer are copyright by the author.

CONTENTS

7   *Ballads of the Old Days*   235

8   *Folk Tales of Our Times*   269

Introduction

THE MAGIC CIRCLE

Long before the printed word, there were stories. When the day's hunt was over, everyone clustered around the fire and called for the storyteller. He related tales he had heard, and wove new ones to celebrate a battle or a hero. Sometimes the excitement of the telling lifted the story into song. The listeners, spellbound, clapped with the rhythm and danced out the action, forgetting themselves and their fear of the night in the story's sorcery. For the stories made magic, and those who listened were part of a magic circle.

The fire no longer burns to warm and bring us together — our modern caves and castles are steam-heated — but the magic has not died. The old spell is cast every time a tale is told or retold. And the enchantment is strongest when the flow of the tale is increased by the accent of verse, by the beat of rhythm and the ring of rhyme.

Every poem in this book has been touched by this enchantment. In these pages are story-poems of adventure, gallant and ghostly. Here, told as only poets can tell them, are legends as spine-tingling as a creaking door, tales of folk heroes and fabulous creatures, of wars and warriors. Humor is here, too, not only in the section called " All In Fun," but waiting to be found in the least expected places. And here are poem-portraits of people, real and imaginary, over whom the poet has waved *his wand until they come alive for you in all their fascinating differences.*

Reading these poems, you can imagine the glow of an ancient fire, and the people ringed around . . . listening . . . singing . . . dreaming. With them, you will fall under the storyteller's spell and share experiences in strange and unknown worlds. You will have joined the magic circle.

L. U.

THE MAGIC CIRCLE

1
STRANGE
TALES

The Ballad of the Harp-Weaver

Poets of all times and countries have been especially fond of two themes: fantasy and love. In the following poem both themes are combined by a famous poet of our own time, Edna St. Vincent Millay. In a fantasy that is simple yet strange, like a fairy tale, she literally weaves a story of mother-love.

" Son," said my mother,
　　When I was knee-high,
" You've need of clothes to cover you,
　　And not a rag have I.

" There's nothing in the house　　　　　　5
　　To make a boy breeches,
Nor shears to cut a cloth with
　　Nor thread to take stitches.

" There's nothing in the house
　　But a loaf-end of rye,　　　　　　　　10
And a harp with a woman's head
　　Nobody will buy,"
　　And she began to cry.

That was in the early fall.
  When came the late fall,   15
" Son," she said, " the sight of you
  Makes your mother's blood crawl, —

" Little skinny shoulder-blades
  Sticking through your clothes!
And where you'll get a jacket from   20
  God above knows.

" It's lucky for me, lad,
  Your daddy's in the ground,
And can't see the way I let
  His son go around! "   25
  And she made a queer sound.

That was in the late fall.
  When the winter came,
I'd not a pair of breeches
  Nor a shirt to my name.   30

I couldn't go to school,
  Or out of doors to play.
And all the other little boys
  Passed our way.

" Son," said my mother,   35
  " Come, climb into my lap,
And I'll chafe your little bones
  While you take a nap."

And, oh, but we were silly
  For half an hour or more,   40

Me with my long legs
   Dragging on the floor,

A-rock-rock-rocking
   To a mother-goose rhyme!
Oh, but we were happy   45
   For half an hour's time!

But there was I, a great boy,
   And what would folks say
To hear my mother singing me
   To sleep all day,   50
   In such a daft way?

Men say the winter
   Was bad that year;
Fuel was scarce,
   And food was dear.   55

A wind with a wolf's head
   Howled about our door,
And we burned up the chairs
   And sat upon the floor.

All that was left us   60
   Was a chair we couldn't break,
And the harp with a woman's head
   Nobody would take,
   For song or pity's sake.

The night before Christmas   65
   I cried with the cold,
I cried myself to sleep
   Like a two-year-old.

And in the deep night
   I felt my mother rise,
And stare down upon me   70
   With love in her eyes.

I saw my mother sitting
   On the one good chair,
A light falling on her   75
   From I couldn't tell where,

Looking nineteen,
   And not a day older,
And the harp with a woman's head
   Leaned against her shoulder.   80

Her thin fingers, moving
   In the thin, tall strings,
Were weav-weav-weaving
   Wonderful things.

Many bright threads,   85
   From where I couldn't see,
Were running through the harp-strings
   Rapidly,

And gold threads whistling
   Through my mother's hand.
I saw the web grow,   90
   And the pattern expand.

She wove a child's jacket,
   And when it was done
She laid it on the floor
   And wove another one.   95

She wove a red cloak
    So regal to see,
"She's made it for a king's son,"
    I said, " and not for me."   100
    But I knew it was for me.

She wove a pair of breeches
    Quicker than that!
She wove a pair of boots
    And a little cocked hat.   105

She wove a pair of mittens,
    She wove a little blouse,
She wove all night
    In the still, cold house.

She sang as she worked,   110
    And the harp-strings spoke;
Her voice never faltered, .
    And the thread never broke.
    And when I awoke, —

There sat my mother   115
    With the harp against her shoulder,
Looking nineteen
    And not a day older,

A smile about her lips,
    And a light about her head,   120
And her hands in the harp-strings
    Frozen dead.

And piled up beside her
  And toppling to the skies,
Were the clothes of a king's son,
  Just my size.

EDNA ST. VINCENT MILLAY

The Lady

Imagine a darkened inn on a lonely road, two centuries ago. Imagine that a lady is left alone in the inn. Who lurks in the darkness? What do these silent ones seek? Even as she is threatened by danger, whether real or imagined, the lady shows courage in her noble and haughty manner.

The candle is out,
it has crashed to the floor,
she follows the wall
to find the door.

Her petticoats hiss   5
with a hiss of fear,
a path of sound
for a sensitive ear.

When she puts out her hand,
her breath gives a catch,   10
fingers are there
instead of a latch!

When she reaches back
lest she should fall,
a body is there
instead of a wall!   15

What use to scream
so sole alone,
what use to struggle
against the unknown?   **20**

" Very well," she said
imperiously,
" Pray light the sconces
so we may see.

" Here are my pearls,   **25**
and here my rings.
And take off your hats,
you filthy things! "

ELIZABETH COATSWORTH

The Code

Because he has lived in rural New England most of his life, Robert Frost knows country folk and country ways better than any other modern poet. Using the language of everyday speech, he makes poems out of conversation; his poetry is full of people talking, picking apples, mending walls, building chimneys, and telling their country stories. Here is a story told by a hired hand. Its near-tragedy reveals that a good worker can be told what to do, but he resents being told two things: how to do the job better and how to do it faster.

There were three in the meadow by the brook
Gathering up windrows, piling cocks of hay,
With an eye always lifted toward the west
Where an irregular sun-bordered cloud
Darkly advanced with a perpetual dagger   5

Flickering across its bosom. Suddenly
One helper, thrusting pitchfork in the ground,
Marched himself off the field and home. One stayed.
The town-bred farmer failed to understand.

" What is there wrong? "

" Something you just now said. "   10

" What did I say? "

" About our taking pains. "

" To cock the hay? — because it's going to shower?
I said that more than half an hour ago.
I said it to myself as much as you."

" You didn't know. But James is one big fool.   15
He thought you meant to find fault with his work.
That's what the average farmer would have meant.
James would take time, of course, to chew it over
Before he acted: he's just got round to act."

" He is a fool if that's the way he takes me."   20

" Don't let it bother you. You've found out something.
The hand that knows his business won't be told
To do work better or faster — those two things.
I'm as particular as anyone:
Most likely I'd have served you just the same.   25
But I know you don't understand our ways.
You were just talking what was in your mind,
What was in all our minds, and you weren't hinting.
Tell you a story of what happened once:
I was up here in Salem at a man's   30
Named Sanders with a gang of four or five
Doing the haying. No one liked the boss.
He was one of the kind sports call a spider,
All wiry arms and legs that spread out wavy
From a humped body nigh as big's a biscuit   35
But work! that man could work, especially
If by so doing he could get more work
Out of his hired help. I'm not denying
He was hard on himself. I couldn't find
That he kept any hours — not for himself.   40
Daylight and lantern-light were one to him:
I've heard him pounding in the barn all night.
But what he liked was someone to encourage.
Them that he couldn't lead he'd get behind

And drive, the way you can, you know, in mowing —   45
Keep at their heels and threaten to mow their legs off.
I'd seen about enough of his bulling tricks
(We call that bulling). I'd been watching him.
So when he paired off with me in the hayfield
To load the load, thinks I, Look out for trouble.   50
I built the load and topped it off; old Sanders
Combed it down with a rake and says, 'O.K.'
Everything went well till we reached the barn
With a big jag to empty in a bay.
You understand that meant the easy job   55
For the man up on top of throwing *down*
The hay and rolling it off wholesale,
Where on a mow it would have been slow lifting.
You wouldn't think a fellow'd need much urging
Under those circumstances, would you now?   60
But the old fool seizes his fork in both hands,
And looking up bewhiskered out of the pit,
Shouts like an army captain, 'Let her come!'
Thinks I, D'ye mean it? 'What was that you said?'
I asked out loud, so's there'd be no mistake,   65
' Did you say, Let her come?' ' Yes, let her come.'
He said it over, but he said it softer.
Never you say a thing like that to a man,
Not if he values what he is. God, I'd as soon
Murdered him as left out his middle name.   70
I'd built the load and knew right where to find it.
Two or three forkfuls I picked lightly round for
Like meditating, and then I just dug in
And dumped the rackful on him in ten lots.
I looked over the side once in the dust   75
And caught sight of him treading-water-like,
Keeping his head above. ' Damn ye,' I says,

' That gets ye! ' He squeaked like a squeezed rat.
That was the last I saw or heard of him.
I cleaned the rack and drove out to cool off.   80
As I sat mopping hayseed from my neck,
And sort of waiting to be asked about it,
One of the boys sings out, ' Where's the old man? '
' I left him in the barn under the hay.
If ye want him, ye can go and dig him out.'   85
They realized from the way I swabbed my neck
More than was needed something must be up.

They headed for the barn; I stayed where I was.
They told me afterward. First they forked hay,
A lot of it, out into the barn floor.   90
Nothing! They listened for him. Not a rustle.
I guess they thought I'd spiked him in the temple
Before I buried him, or I couldn't have managed.
They excavated more. ' Go keep his wife
Out of the barn.' Someone looked in a window,   95
And curse me if he wasn't in the kitchen
Slumped way down in a chair, with both his feet
Against the stove, the hottest day that summer.
He looked so clean disgusted from behind
There was no one that dared to stir him up,   100
Or let him know that he was being looked at.
Apparently I hadn't buried him
(I may have knocked him down); but my just trying
To bury him had hurt his dignity.
He had gone to the house so's not to meet me.   105
He kept away from us all afternoon.
We tended to his hay. We saw him out
After a while picking peas in his garden:
He couldn't keep away from doing something."

" Weren't you relieved to find he wasn't dead? "   110

" No! and yet I don't know — it's hard to say.
I went about to kill him fair enough."

" You took an awkward way. Did he discharge you? "

" Discharge me? No! He knew I did just right."

ROBERT FROST

Old Christmas

*In the Kentucky hill country there is a superstition that strange,
unnatural things may happen on " Old Christmas," which accord-
ing to a calendar no longer in use makes Christmas Day fall twelve
days after its present date. The setting of the following poem is one
Old Christmas when two women meet in the gray light of morning.
Lomey Carter and Sally Anne Barton belong to feuding families
but they meet agreeably enough. In fact, the story begins so simply
that you may not be prepared for the sudden twists to come.*

" Where you coming from, Lomey Carter,
    So airly over the snow?
And what's them pretties you got in your hand,
    And where you aiming to go?

" Step in, Honey: Old Christmas morning   5
    I ain't got nothing much;
Maybe a bite of sweetness and corn bread,
    A little ham meat and such.

" But come in, Honey! Sally Anne Barton's
    Hungering after your face.   10

Wait till I light my candle up:
　　Set down! There's your old place.

" Now where you been so airly this morning? "
　　" *Graveyard, Sally Anne.*
Up by the trace in the salt lick meadows　　　　15
　　Where Taulbe kilt my man."

" Taulbe ain't to home this morning . . .
　　I can't scratch up a light:
Dampness gets on the heads of the matches;
　　But I'll blow up the embers bright."　　　　20

" *Needn't trouble. I won't be stopping:*
　　Going a long ways still."
" You didn't see nothing, Lomey Carter,
　　Up on the graveyard hill? "

" *What should I see there, Sally Anne Barton?* "　　25
　　" Well, sperits do walk last night."
" *There were an elder bush a-blooming*
　　While the moon still give some light."

" Yes, elder bushes, they bloom, Old Christmas,
　　And critters kneel down in their straw.　　　30
Anything else up in the graveyard? "
　　" *One thing more I saw:*

" *I saw my man with his head all bleeding*
　　Where Taulbe's shot went through."
" What did he say? " " *He stooped and kissed me.*"　35
　　" What did he say to you? "

" *Said, Lord Jesus forguv your Taulbe;*
  But he told me another word;
He said it soft when he stooped and kissed me.
  That were the last I heard."   40

" *Taulbe ain't to home this morning.*"
  " *I know that, Sally Anne,*
For I kilt him, coming down through the meadow
  Where Taulbe kilt my man.

" *I met him upon the meadow trace*   45
  When the moon were fainting fast,
And I had my dead man's rifle gun
  And kilt him as he come past."

" *But I heard two shots.*" " *'Twas his was second:*
  He shot me 'fore he died: 50
You'll find us at daybreak, Sally Anne Barton:
  I'm laying there dead at his side."

ROY HELTON

Peter and John

" Peter and John " is a fantasy centering about the twelve apostles who " gathered unto Jesus and told him all things, both what they had done and what they had taught." Their task was to heal the sick and spread the Gospel, although one of the twelve, Judas Iscariot, was false to his trust and betrayed his Lord. The poem deals with a time when the apostles were still united in a close brotherhood — and therefore Peter's dream about Judas is a forecast of things to come. It is also a prophecy about Peter himself, who was to fail his Master when he was in trouble. " Before the cock crow, thou shalt deny me thrice," said Jesus, and Peter had replied: " Though I should die with thee, yet I will not deny thee." But, at the moment of trial, Peter lost his courage.

Twelve good friends
Walked under the leaves,
Binding the ends
Of the barley sheaves.

Peter and John   5
Lay down to sleep,
Pillowed upon
A haymaker's heap.

John and Peter
Lay down to dream.   10
The air was sweeter
Than honey and cream.

Peter was bred
In the salty cold.
His hair was red   15
And his eyes were gold.

John had a mouth
Like a wing bent down.
His brow was smooth
And his eyes were brown.   20

Peter to slumber
Sank like a stone,
Of all their number
The bravest one.

John more slowly   25
Composed himself,
Young and holy
Among the Twelve.

John as he slept
Cried out in grief,   30
Turned and wept
On the golden leaf:

" Peter, Peter,
Give me a sign!
This was a bitter   35
Dream of mine —

" Bitter as aloes
It parched my tongue.
Upon the gallows
My life was hung.   40

" Sharp it seemed
As a bloody sword.
Peter, I dreamed
I was Christ the Lord! "

Peter turned   45
To holy Saint John;
His body burned
In the falling sun.

In the falling sun
He burned like flame: 50
" John, Saint John,
I have dreamed the same!

" My bones were hung
On an elder tree;
Bells were rung   55
Over Galilee.

" A silver penny
Sealed each of my eyes.
Many and many
A cock crew thrice."   60

When Peter's word
Was spoken and done,
" Were you Christ the Lord
In your dream? " said John.

" No," said the other,   65
" That I was not.
I was our brother
Iscariot."

ELINOR WYLIE

The Listeners

*This poem and the one that follows suggest more than they say. A
story is told in each of the poems, but it is told indirectly, in whispers and words which seem to be holding something back. In both
poems you will be thrilled by the sense of something half revealed,
half concealed. Both rouse your imagination to a pitch of pure excitement. " The Listeners " can be interpreted in many different
ways. It may be a spirit returning to the scene of strange happen-
ings. It may be the story of a heroic figure surrounded by threaten-
ing shadows, as the traveler flings his challenge to whoever is listening: " Tell them I came, and no one answered, that I kept my
word." We feel the chill, the sinister silence and creeping darkness,
though we do not know what has brought the traveler there.*

" Is there anybody there? " said the Traveler,
    Knocking on the moonlit door;
And his horse in the silence champed the grasses
    Of the forest's ferny floor.

And a bird flew up out of the turret,   5
   Above the Traveler's head:
And he smote upon the door again a second time;
   " Is there anybody there? " he said.
But no one descended to the Traveler;
   No head from the leaf-fringed sill   10
Leaned over and looked into his gray eyes,
   Where he stood perplexed and still.
But only a host of phantom listeners
   That dwelt in the lone house then
Stood listening in the quiet of the moonlight   15
   To that voice from the world of men:
Stood thronging the faint moonbeams on the dark stair
   That goes down to the empty hall,
Hearkening in an air stirred and shaken
   By the lonely Traveler's call.   20
And he felt in his heart their strangeness,
   Their stillness answering his cry,
While his horse moved, cropping the dark turf,
   'Neath the starred and leafy sky;
For he suddenly smote on the door, even   25
   Louder, and lifted his head: —
" Tell them I came, and no one answered,
   That I kept my word," he said.
Never the least stir made the listeners,
   Though every word he spake   30
Fell echoing through the shadowiness of the still house
   From the one man left awake:
Aye, they heard his foot upon the stirrup,
   And the sound of iron on stone,
And how the silence surged softly backward,   35
   When the plunging hoofs were gone.

                    WALTER DE LA MARE

Ballad

O what is that sound which so thrills the ear
  Down in the valley drumming, drumming?
Only the scarlet soldiers, dear,
  The soldiers coming.

O what is that light I see flashing so clear   5
  Over the distance brightly, brightly?
Only the sun on their weapons, dear,
  As they step lightly.

O what are they doing with all that gear;
  What are they doing this morning, this morning?   10
Only the usual maneuvers, dear,
  Or perhaps a warning.

O why have they left the road down there;
  Why are they suddenly wheeling, wheeling?
Perhaps a change in the orders, dear;   15
  Why are you kneeling?

O haven't they stopped for the doctor's care;
  Haven't they reined their horses, their horses?
Why, they are none of them wounded, dear,
  None of these forces.   20

O is it the parson they want, with white hair;
  Is it the parson, is it, is it?
No, they are passing his gateway, dear,
  Without a visit.

O it must be the farmer who lives so near,   25
    It must be the farmer, so cunning, cunning;
They have passed the farm already, dear,
    And now they are running.

O where are you going? stay with me here.
    Were the vows you swore me deceiving, deceiving?   30
No, I promised to love you, my dear,
    But I must be leaving.

O it's broken the lock and splintered the door,
    O it's the gate where they're turning, turning;
Their feet are heavy on the floor   35
    And their eyes are burning.

W. H. AUDEN

The Heart

In Brittany there lived a lad;
    (*Listen, my love*)
And a girl as fair as she was bad.
    (*O, my own.*)

He told her by day of his constant pain;   5
    (*Listen, my love*)
He told her at night and he told her in vain.
    (*O, my own.*)

She laughed at his prayers till the lad grew wild;
    (*Listen, my love*)   10
She mocked him and said, " You are only a child."
    (*O, my own.*)

" If you were a man as I've heard you boast,
  (*Listen, my love*)
You'd bring me the thing you cherish the most." 15
  (*O, my own.*)

" If you were in love so passionately,
  (*Listen, my love*)
You'd bring your mother's heart to me."
  (*O, my own.*) 20

The lad went home, the night was black;
  (*Listen, my love*)
He slew his mother and hurried back.
  (*O, my own.*)

And as he hurried with tight-clenched hand, 25
  (*Listen, my love*)
He fell, and the heart rolled over the sand
  (*O, my own.*)

His mother's heart — he heard it call:
  (*Listen, my love*) 30
" Are you hurt, my lad, are you hurt at all?
  O, my own! "

FROM THE FRENCH
Adapted by Louis Untermeyer

Kubla Khan

*Here is a great poem made of music, magic, and mystery. Even its
creation was mysterious, for the image of the stately palace dome,
the strange walls and towers, the weird caves of ice, and the meas-*

ureless caverns came to the poet in a dream. As soon as he awoke,
Coleridge began to put his impressions into words but, after a mag-
nificent beginning, he was interrupted by a visitor. Later, when he
tried to resume writing, he could not recapture the mood, and the
poem was never finished. Kubla Khan was a real person, a powerful
Oriental emperor, but "Kubla Khan" is visionary rather than his-
torical, and it is as a dream that the poem should be read.

In Xanadu did Kubla Khan
   A stately pleasure-dome decree:
Where Alph, the sacred river, ran
Through caverns measureless to man
   Down to a sunless sea.   5
So twice five miles of fertile ground
With walls and towers were girdled round:
And there were gardens bright with sinuous rills,
Where blossomed many an incense-bearing tree;
And here were forests ancient as the hills,   10
Enfolding sunny spots of greenery.

But O! that deep romantic chasm which slanted
Down the green hill athwart a cedarn cover!
A savage place! as holy and enchanted
As e'er beneath a waning moon was haunted   15
By woman wailing for her demon-lover!
And from this chasm, with ceaseless turmoil seething,
As if this Earth in fast thick pants were breathing,
A mighty fountain momently was forced,
Amid whose swift half-intermitted burst   20
Huge fragments vaulted like rebounding hail,
Or chaffy grain beneath the thresher's flail:
And 'mid these dancing rocks at once and ever
It flung up momently the sacred river.
Five miles meandering with a mazy motion   25

Through wood and dale the sacred river ran,
Then reached the caverns measureless to man,
And sank in tumult to a lifeless ocean:
And 'mid this tumult Kubla heard from far
Ancestral voices prophesying war!   30

    The shadow of the dome of pleasure
    Floated midway on the waves;

    Where was heard the mingled measure
    From the fountain and the caves.
It was a miracle of rare device,   35
A sunny pleasure-dome with caves of ice!

    A damsel with a dulcimer
    In a vision once I saw:
    It was an Abyssinian maid,
    And on her dulcimer she played,   40
    Singing of Mount Abora.
    Could I revive within me
    Her symphony and song,

To such a deep delight 'twould win me
That, with music loud and long,   45
I would build that dome in air,
That sunny dome! those caves of ice!

And all who heard should see them there,
And all should cry, Beware! Beware!
His flashing eyes, his floating hair!   50
Weave a circle round him thrice,
And close your eyes with holy dread,
For he on honey-dew hath fed,
And drunk the milk of Paradise.

SAMUEL TAYLOR COLERIDGE

The Skeleton in Armor

In Massachusetts there was found about a century ago the grave of what is believed to have been an ancient Viking warrior. When "the skeleton in armor" was discovered, the poet Longfellow and many others considered it additional evidence that Scandinavian seafarers had come to America long before Columbus. They guessed at a connection between the skeleton and an ancient tower of stone in Newport, Rhode Island, which might have been built by Norsemen.

Longfellow's imagination was kindled and he wrote this fanciful history of adventure to explain the tower and the grave. In the poem you will feel the surge and rush of the sea, as the old Viking describes his early days when he tamed fierce birds like the gerfalcon and when he sat drinking with wild Norse fighters, the Berserks. Longfellow has his warrior describe how he came to America with his captive bride when his ship was driven by a storm round "the gusty Skaw," a point off northern Denmark, and westward to the undiscovered land.

" Speak! speak! thou fearful guest!
Who, with thy hollow breast
Still in rude armor drest,
 Comest to daunt me!
Wrapped not in Eastern balms,   5
But with thy fleshless palms
Stretched, as if asking alms,
 Why dost thou haunt me? "

Then, from those cavernous eyes
Pale flashes seemed to rise,   10
As when the Northern skies
 Gleam in December;
And, like the water's flow
Under December's snow,
Came a dull voice of woe   15
 From the heart's chamber.

" I was a Viking old!
My deeds, though manifold,
No Skald in song has told,
 No Saga taught thee!   20
Take heed, that in thy verse
Thou dost the tale rehearse,
Else dread a dead man's curse;
 For this I sought thee.

" Far in the Northern Land,   25
By the wild Baltic's strand,
I, with my childish hand,
 Tamed the gerfalcon;
And, with my skates fast-bound,

Skimmed the half-frozen Sound,   30
That the poor whimpering hound
    Trembled to walk on.

" Oft to his frozen lair
Tracked I the grisly bear,
While from my path the hare   35
    Fled like a shadow;
Oft through the forest dark
Followed the werewolf's bark,
Until the soaring lark
    Sang from the meadow.   40

" But when I older grew.
Joining a corsair's crew,
O'er the dark sea I flew
    With the marauders.
Wild was the life we led;   45
Many the souls that sped,
Many the hearts that bled,
    By our stern orders.

" Many a wassail-bout
Wore the long Winter out   50
Often our midnight shout
    Set the cocks crowing,
As we the Berserk's tale
Measured in cups of ale,
Draining the oaken pail,   55
    Filled to o'erflowing.

" Once as I told in glee
Tales of the stormy sea,

Soft eyes did gaze on me,
    Burning yet tender;   60
And as the white stars shine
On the dark Norway pine,
On that dark heart of mine
    Fell their soft splendor.'

" I wooed the blue-eyed maid,   65
Yielding, yet half afraid,
And in the forest's shade
    Our vows were plighted.
Under its loosened vest
Fluttered her little breast,   70
Like birds within their nest
    By the hawk frighted.

" Bright in her father's hall
Shields gleamed upon the wall,
Loud sang the minstrels all,   75
    Chanting his glory;
When of old Hildebrand
I asked his daughter's hand,
Mute did the minstrels stand
    To hear my story.   80

" While the brown ale he quaffed,
Loud then the champion laughed.
And as the wind gusts waft
    The sea-foam brightly,
So the loud laugh of scorn,   85
Out of those lips unshorn,
From the deep drinking-horn
    Blew the foam lightly.

" She was a Prince's child,
I but a Viking wild,   90
And though she blushed and smiled,
    I was discarded!
Should not the dove so white ·
Follow the sea-mew's flight,
Why did they leave that night   95
    Her nest unguarded?

" Scarce had I put to sea,
Bearing the maid with me, —
Fairest of all was she
    Among the Norsemen! —   100
When on the white sea-strand,
Waving his armèd hand,
Saw we old Hildebrand,
    With twenty horsemen.

" Then launched they to the blast,   105
Bent like a reed each mast,
Yet we were gaining fast,
    When the wind failed us;
And with a sudden flaw
Came round the gusty Skaw,   110
So that our foe we saw
    Laugh as he hailed us.

" And as to catch the gale
Round veered the flapping sail,
Death! was the helmsman's hail,   115
    Death without quarter!
Mid-ships with iron keel
Struck we her ribs of steel;
Down her black hulk did reel
    Through the black water!   120

" As with his wings aslant,
Sails the fierce cormorant,
Seeking some rocky haunt,
    With his prey laden,
So toward the open main,   125
Beating to sea again,
Through the wild hurricane
    Bore I the maiden.

" Three weeks we westward bore,
And when the storm was o'er,   130
Cloudlike we saw the shore
    Stretching to leeward;
There for my lady's bower
Built I the lofty tower,
Which, to this very hour,   135
    Stands looking seaward.

" There lived we many years;
Time dried the maiden's tears;
She had forgot her fears,
    She was a mother;   140
Death closed her mild blue eyes,
Under that tower she lies;
Ne'er shall the sun arise
    On such another!

" Still grew my bosom then,   145
Still as a stagnant fen!
Hateful to me were men,
    The sunlight hateful!
In the vast forest here,
Clad in my warlike gear,   150
Fell I upon my spear,
    O, death was grateful!

" Thus, seamed with many scars
Bursting these prison bars,
Up to its native stars   155
    My soul ascended.
There from the flowing bowl
Deep drinks the warrior's soul,
Skoal! to the Northland! *Skoal!* "
    — Thus the tale ended.

HENRY WADSWORTH LONGFELLOW

La Belle Dame sans Merci

The ballad of " True Thomas " (page 242) is about a man be-
witched by an immortal, or supernatural, creature. John Keats's
" La Belle Dame sans Merci " (" The Beautiful Woman without
Mercy ") is a variation of that old story-poem. In both poems there
is the same " plot ": the fair woman, who is an enchantress, falls in
love with a man and keeps him captive for years.

" O what can ail thee, knight-at-arms,
    Alone and palely loitering?
The sedge is withered from the lake,
    And no birds sing.

" O what can ail thee, knight-at-arms,   5
    So haggard and so woe-begone?
The squirrel's granary is full,
    And the harvest's done.

" I see a lily on thy brow
    With anguish moist and fever dew;   10
And on thy cheek a fading rose
    Fast withereth too."

" I met a lady in the meads,
    Full beautiful — a faery's child;
Her hair was long, her foot was light, 15
    And her eyes were wild.

" I made a garland for her head,
    And bracelets too, and fragrant zone;
She looked at me as she did love,
    And made sweet moan. 20

" I set her on my pacing steed
    And nothing else saw all day long,
For sideways would she lean, and sing
    A faery's song.

" She found me roots of relish sweet, 25
    And honey wild and manna dew,
And sure in language strange she said,
    ' I love thee true! '

" She took me to her elfin grot,
    And there she wept and sighed full sore; 30
And there I shut her wild, wild eyes
    With kisses four.

" And there she lulled me asleep,
    And there I dreamed — Ah! woe betide!
The latest dream I ever dreamed 35
    On the cold hill's side.

" I saw pale kings, and princes too,
    Pale warriors, death-pale were they all;
Who cried — ' La Belle Dame sans Merci
    Hath thee in thrall! ' 40

" I saw their starved lips in the gloam
　　With horrid warning gapèd wide,
And I awoke and found me here
　　On the cold hill's side.

" And this is why I sojourn here   45
　　Alone and palely loitering,
Though the sedge is withered from the lake,
　　And no birds sing."

JOHN KEATS

The Erl-King

Who ride by night through the woodland so wild?
It is the fond father embracing his child;
And close the boy nestles within his loved arm.
To hold himself fast, and to keep himself warm.

" O father, see yonder! see yonder! " he says.   5
" My boy, upon what dost thou fearfully gaze? "
" O, 'tis the Erl-King with his crown and his shroud."
" No, my son, it is but a dark wreath of the cloud."

　　　　　(*The Erl-King speaks*)
"O come and go with me, thou loveliest child;
By many a gay sport shall thy time be beguiled;   10
My mother keeps for thee full many a toy,
And many a fine flower shall she pluck for my boy."

" O father, my father, and did you not hear
The Erl-King whisper so low in my ear? "
" Be still, my heart's darling — my child, be at ease.   15
It was but the wild blast as it sung through the trees."

(Erl-King)

" O wilt thou go with me, thou loveliest boy?
My daughter shall tend thee with care and with joy;
She shall bear thee so lightly through wet and through wild,
And press thee, and kiss thee, and sing to my child."   20

" O father, my father, and saw you not plain
The Erl-King's pale daughter glide past through the rain? "
" O yes, my loved treasure, I knew it full soon;
It was the gray willow that danced to the moon."

(Erl-King)

" O come and go with me, no longer delay,   25
Or else, silly child, I will drag thee away."
" O father! O father! now, now, keep your hold,
The Erl-King has seized me — his grasp is so cold! "

Sore trembled the father; he spurred through the wild,
Clasping close to his bosom his shuddering child.   30
He reaches his dwelling in doubt and in dread,
But clasped to his bosom, the infant lies dead.

FROM THE GERMAN OF GOETHE
Translated by Walter Scott

Danny Deever

*In tightly packed questions and answers two soldiers are discussing
a crime committed by a fellow-soldier, Danny Deever, who quar-
reled with his comrade and shot him while he slept. One of the
speakers is timid and sympathetic; the other is older, more experi-
enced, and thicker skinned. Against a tragic background, in ballad-
like verses, two people are revealed vividly and unforgettably.*

" What are the bugles blowin' for? " said Files-on-Parade.

" To turn you out, to turn you out," the Color-Sergeant said.

" What makes you look so white, so white? " said Files-on-Parade.

" I'm dreadin' what I've got to watch," the Color-Sergeant said.

 For they're hangin' Danny Deever, you can 'ear the Dead March play,   5

 The regiment's in 'ollow square — they're hangin' him today;

 They've taken of his buttons off an' cut his stripes away,

 An' they're hangin' Danny Deever in the mornin'.

" What makes the rear-rank breathe so 'ard? " said Files-on-Parade.

" It's bitter cold, it's bitter cold," the Color-Sergeant said. 10

" What makes that front-rank man fall down? " says Files-on-Parade.

" A touch of sun, a touch of sun," the Color-Sergeant said.

 They are hangin' Danny Deever, they are marchin' of 'im round.

 They 'ave 'alted Danny Deever by 'is coffin on the ground:

 An 'e'll swing in 'arf a minute for a sneakin' shootin' hound —   15

 O they're hangin' Danny Deever in the mornin'!

" 'Is cot was right-'and cot to mine," said Files-on-Parade.

" 'E's sleepin' out an' far tonight," the Color-Sergeant said.

" I've drunk 'is beer a score o' times," said Files-on-Parade.

" 'E's drinkin' bitter beer alone," the Color-Sergeant said. 20

 They are hangin' Danny Deever, you must mark 'im to 'is place,

For 'e shot a comrade sleepin' — you must look 'im in the
    face;
Nine 'undred of 'is county an' the regiment's disgrace,
While they're hangin' Danny Deever in the mornin'.

" What's that so black agin the sun? " said Files-on-Parade.
" It's Danny fightin' 'ard for life," the Color-Sergeant said.   26
" What's that that whimpers over'ead? " said Files-on-Parade.
" It's Danny's soul that's passin' now," the Color-Sergeant said.
    For they're done with Danny Deever, you can 'ear the
        quickstep play,   30
    The regiment's in column, an' they're marchin' us
        away;
    Ho! the young recruits are shakin', an' they'll want their
        beer today,
    After hangin' Danny Deever in the mornin'.

RUDYARD KIPLING

The Shooting of Dan McGrew

*A half-century ago there was perhaps no rougher, more dangerous
place in the world than the Yukon territory in Alaska. Thousands
of gold-seekers rushed into towns like Nome to seek their fortunes.
Among them was Robert W. Service, who turned what he saw into
rousing, adventurous poetry.*

A bunch of the boys were whooping it up in the Malamute
    saloon;
The kid that handles the music-box was hitting a jag-time
    tune;
Back of the bar, in a solo game, sat Dangerous Dan McGrew,
And watching his luck was his light-o'-love, the lady that's
    known as Lou.

When out of the night, which was fifty below, and into the
    din and the glare,   5
There stumbled a miner fresh from the creeks, dog-dirty, and
    loaded for bear.
He looked like a man with a foot in the grave and scarcely the
    strength of a louse,
Yet he tilted a poke of dust on the bar, and he called for
    drinks for the house.
There was none could place the stranger's face, though we
    searched ourselves for a clue;
But we drank his health, and the last to drink was Dangerous
    Dan McGrew.   10

There's men that somehow just grip your eyes, and hold them
    hard like a spell;
And such was he, and he looked to me like a man who had
    lived in hell;
With a face most hair, and the dreary stare of a dog whose day
    is done,
As he watered the green stuff in his glass, and the drops fell
    one by one.
Then I got to figgering who he was, and wondering what he'd
    do,   .   15
And I turned my head — and there watching him was the
    lady that's known as Lou.

His eyes went rubbering round the room, and he seemed in a
    kind of daze,
Till at last that old piano fell in the way of his wandering gaze.
The rag-time kid was having a drink; there was no one else on
    the stool,
So the stranger stumbles across the room, and flops down there
    like a fool.   20

In a buckskin shirt that was glazed with dirt he sat, and I saw
    him sway;
Then he clutched the keys with his talon hands — my God!
    but that man could play.

Were you ever out in the Great Alone, when the moon was
    awful clear,
And the icy mountains hemmed you in with a silence you
    most could *hear*;
With only the howl of a timber wolf, and you camped there
    in the cold,   25
A half-dead thing in a stark, dead world, clean mad for the
    muck called gold;
While high overhead, green, yellow and red, the North Lights
    swept in bars? —
Then you've a hunch what the music meant . . . hunger and
    night and the stars.

And hunger not of the belly kind, that's banished with bacon
    and beans,
But the gnawing hunger of lonely men for a home and all that
    it means;   30
For a fireside far from the cares that are, four walls and a roof
    above;
But oh! so cramful of cozy joy, and crowned with a woman's
    love —
A woman dearer than all the world, and true as Heaven is
    true —
(God! how ghastly she looks through her rouge,— the lady
    that's known as Lou.)

Then on a sudden the music changed, so soft that you scarce
    could hear;   35

But you felt that your life had been looted clean of all that it
    once held dear;

That someone had stolen the woman you loved; that her love
    was a devil's lie;

That your guts were gone, and the best for you was to crawl
    away and die.

'Twas the crowning cry of a heart's despair, and it thrilled you
    through and through —

" I guess I'll make it a spread misere," said Dangerous Dan
    McGrew.   40

The music almost died away . . . then it burst like a pent-up
    flood;

And it seemed to say, " Repay, repay," and my eyes were blind
    with blood.

The thought came back of an ancient wrong, and it stung like
    a frozen lash,

And the lust awoke to kill, to kill . . . then the music stopped
    with a crash,

And the stranger turned, and his eyes they burned in a most
    peculiar way;   45

In a buckskin shirt that was glazed with dirt he sat, and I saw
    him sway;

Then his lips went in in a kind of grin, and he spoke, and his
    voice was calm,

And " Boys," says he, " you don't know me, and none of you
    care a damn;

But I want to state, and my words are straight, and I'll bet my
    poke they're true,

That one of you is a hound of hell . . . and that one is Dan
    McGrew."   50

Then I ducked my head, and the lights went out, and two guns
    blazed in the dark,

And a woman screamed, and the lights went up, and two men
  lay stiff and stark.

Pitched on his head, and pumped full of lead, was Dangerous
  Dan McGrew,
While the man from the creeks lay clutched to the breast of
  the lady that's known as Lou.

These are the simple facts of the case, and I guess I ought to
  know.   55
They say that the stranger was crazed with " hooch," and I'm
  not denying it's so.

I'm not so wise as the lawyer guys, but strictly between us
   two —
The woman that kissed him and — pinched his poke — was
   the lady that's known as Lou.

ROBERT W. SERVICE

Nightmare Number Three

*These days we hear much about machines and how they are gradu-
ally taking the place of men in industry. For example, a huge cal-
culating machine, called Mark IV, is so sensitive and complex that
it not only solves all kinds of mathematical problems, but also has
a memory! And in this atomic age we hear much of the danger of
machines which, if used for evil, can destroy man. Stephen Vincent
Benét was inspired by the rapid progress of machines — of " thinking" machines and monster robots with mechanical " brains " to
write a series of poems he called " Nightmares." In the following
fantasy he imagines what would happen if the machines that serve
us every day — the telephones, printing presses, cement mixers —
were to revolt against human beings. It is a grim dream.*

We had expected everything but revolt
And I kind of wonder myself when they started thinking —
But there's no dice in that now.
                             I've heard fellows say
They must have planned it for years and maybe they did.
Looking back, you can find little incidents here and there,   5
Like the concrete-mixer in Jersey eating the guy
Or the roto press that printed " Fiddle-dee-dee! "
In a three-color process all over Senator Sloop,
Just as he was making a speech. The thing about that
Was, how could it walk upstairs? But it *was* upstairs,   10
Clicking and mumbling in the Senate Chamber.

They had to knock out the wall to take it away
And the wrecking-crew said it grinned.

                        It was only the best
Machines, of course, the superhuman machines,
The ones we'd built to be better than flesh and bone,   15
But the cars were in it, of course. . . .

                      and they hunted us
Like rabbits through the cramped streets on that Bloody
    Monday,

The Madison Avenue busses leading the charge.
The busses were pretty bad — but I'll not forget
The smash of glass when the Duesenberg left the show-room
And pinned three brokers to the Racquet Club steps,   21
Or the long howl of the horns when they saw the men
    run,
When they saw them looking for holes in the solid ground . . .

I guess they were tired of being ridden in,
And stopped and started by pygmies for silly ends,   25
Of wrapping cheap cigarettes and bad chocolate bars,
Collecting nickels and waving platinum hair,
And letting six million people live in a town.
I guess it was that. I guess they got tired of us
And the whole smell of human hands.

                    But it was a shock   30
'To climb sixteen flights of stairs to Art Zuckow's office
(Nobody took the elevators twice)

And find him strangled to death in a nest of telephones,
The octopus-tendrils waving over his head,
And a sort of quiet humming filling the air . . .   35
Do they eat? . . . There was red . . . But I did not stop to
     look.
And it's lonely, here on the roof.
                                        For a while I thought
That window-cleaner would make it, and keep me company.
But they got him with his own hoist at the sixteenth floor
And dragged him in with a squeal.   40
You see, they co-operate. Well, we taught them that,
And it's fair enough, I suppose. You see, we built them.
We taught them to think for themselves.
It was bound to come. You can see it was bound to come.
And it won't be so bad, in the country. I hate to think   45
Of the reapers, running wild in the Kansas fields,
And the transport planes like hawks on a chickenyard,
But the horses might help. We might make a deal with the
     horses.
At least you've more chance, out there.

                                        And they need us too.
They're bound to realize that when they once calm down.   50
They'll need oil and spare parts and adjustments and tun-
     ing up.
Slaves? Well, in a way, you know, we were slaves before.
There won't be so much real difference — honest there won't.
(I wish I hadn't looked into that beauty-parlor
And seen what was happening there.   55
But those are female machines and a bit high-strung.)
Oh, we'll settle down. We'll arrange it. We'll compromise.
It wouldn't make sense to wipe out the whole human race.
Why, I bet if I went to my old Plymouth now

(Of course, you'd have to do it the tactful way) 60
And said, " Look here! Who got you the swell French horn? "
He wouldn't turn me over to those police cars.
At least I don't *think* he would.
        Oh, it's going to be jake.
There won't be so much real difference — honest, there
  won't —
And I'd go down in a minute and take my chance — 65
I'm a good American and I always liked them —
Except for one small detail that bothers me
And that's the food proposition. Because you see,
The concrete-mixer may have made a mistake,
And it looks like just high spirits. 70
But, if it's got so they like the flavor . . . well . . .

       STEPHEN VINCENT BENÉT

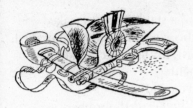

2
GALLANT
DEEDS

The Highwayman

PART I

The wind was a torrent of darkness among the gusty trees,
The moon was a ghostly galleon tossed upon cloudy seas,
The road was a ribbon of moonlight over the purple moor,
And the highwayman came riding —
    Riding — riding —   5
The highwayman came riding, up to the old inn-door.

He'd a French cocked-hat on his forehead, a bunch of lace at
    his chin,
A coat of the claret velvet, and breeches of brown doe-skin;
They fitted with never a wrinkle; his boots were up to the
    thigh!
And he rode with a jeweled twinkle,   10
    His pistol butts a-twinkle,
His rapier hilt a-twinkle, under the jeweled sky.

Over the cobbles he clattered and clashed in the dark inn-yard,
And he tapped with his whip on the shutters, but all was
    locked and barred:
He whistled a tune to the window, and who should be waiting
    there   15
But the landlord's black-eyed daughter,
    Bess, the landlord's daughter,
Plaiting a dark red love-knot into her long black hair.

And dark in the dark old inn-yard a stable-wicket creaked
Where Tim the ostler listened; his face was white and peaked;
His eyes were hollows of madness, his hair like moldy hay,
But he loved the landlord's daughter,   22
      The landlord's red-lipped daughter,
Dumb as a dog he listened, and he heard the robber say —

" One kiss, my bonny sweetheart, I'm after a prize tonight,
But I shall be back with the yellow gold before the morning
    light;   26
Yet, if they press me sharply, and harry me through the day,
Then look for me by moonlight,
      Watch for me by moonlight,
I'll come to thee by moonlight, though hell should bar the
    way."   30

He rose upright in the stirrups; he scarce could reach her hand,
But she loosened her hair i' the casement! His face burned like
    a brand
As the black cascade of perfume came tumbling over his
    breast;
And he kissed its waves in the moonlight,
    (Oh, sweet black waves in the moonlight!)   35
Then he tugged at his rein in the moonlight, and galloped
    away to the West.

PART II

He did not come in the dawning; he did not come at
    noon;
And out o' the tawny sunset, before the rise o' the moon,
When the road was a gipsy's ribbon, looping the purple moor,
A red-coat troop came marching —   40
    Marching — marching —
King George's men came marching, up to the old inn-door.

They said no word to the landlord, they drank his ale instead,
But they gagged his daughter and bound her to the foot of her
    narrow bed;
Two of them knelt at her casement, with muskets at their
    side!   45
There was death at every window;
      And hell at one dark window;
For Bess could see, through her casement, the road that *he*
    would ride.

They had tied her up to attention, with many a sniggering jest;
They had bound a musket beside her, with the barrel beneath
    her breast!   50
" Now keep good watch! " and they kissed her. She heard
    the dead man say —
Look for me by moonlight;
    Watch for me by moonlight;
I'll come to thee by moonlight, though hell should bar the
    way!

She twisted her hands behind her; but all the knots held
    good!   55
She writhed her hands till her fingers were wet with sweat or
    blood!
They stretched and strained in the darkness, and the hours
    crawled by like years,
Till now, on the stroke of midnight,
    Cold, on the stroke of midnight,
The tip of one finger touched it! The trigger at least was hers!

The tip of one finger touched it; she strove no more for the
    rest!   61
Up, she stood up to attention, with the barrel beneath her
    breast,

She would not risk their hearing: she would not strive again;
For the road lay bare in the moonlight;
   Blank and bare in the moonlight;   65
And the blood of her veins in the moonlight throbbed to her
 love's refrain.

Tlot-tlot; tlot-tlot! Had they heard it? The horse-hoofs ringing
 clear;
Tlot-tlot, tlot-tlot, in the distance? Were they deaf that they
 did not hear?
Down the ribbon of moonlight, over the brow of the hill,
The highwayman came riding,   70
   Riding, riding!
The red-coats looked to their priming! She stood up, straight
 and still!

Tlot-tlot, in the frosty silence! *Tlot-tlot,* in the echoing night!
Nearer he came and nearer! Her face was like a light!
Her eyes grew wide for a moment; she drew one last deep
 breath,
                75
Then her finger moved in the moonlight,
   Her musket shattered the moonlight,
Shattered her breast in the moonlight and warned him — with
 her death.

He turned; he spurred to the westward; he did not know who
 stood
Bowed, with her head o'er the musket, drenched with her own
 red blood!   80
Not till the dawn he heard it, his face grew gray to hear
How Bess, the landlord's daughter,
   The landlord's black-eyed daughter,
Had watched for her love in the moonlight, and died in the
 darkness there.

Back he spurred like a madman, shrieking a curse to the sky,
With the white road smoking behind him, and his rapier
    brandished high! 86
Blood-red were his spurs in the golden moon; wine-red was his
    velvet coat,
When they shot him down on the highway,
       Down like a dog on the highway,
And he lay in his blood on the highway, with a bunch of lace
    at his throat. 90

.   .   .   .

And still of a winter's night, they say, when the wind is in the
    trees,
When the moon is a ghostly galleon tossed upon cloudy
    seas,
When the road is a ribbon of moonlight over the purple moor,
A highwayman comes riding —
    Riding — riding — 95
A highwayman comes riding, up to the old inn-door.

Over the cobbles he clatters and clangs in the dark inn-
    yard;
And he taps with his whip on the shutters, but all is locked and
    barred;
He whistles a tune to the window, and who should be waiting
    there
    But the landlord's black-eyed daughter, 100
       Bess, the landlord's daughter,
    Plaiting a dark red love-knot into her long black hair.

ALFRED NOYES

The Ballad of East and West

*Like the best of ballads this tale of India has speed of movement
and an exciting beat. It plunges the reader immediately into the
midst of events, taking him along on a galloping ride, carrying him
through a series of dramatic moments. The poem is also a study of
character — of two men from two types of civilization.*

*When Rudyard Kipling was a young man in India, more than
seventy years ago, the British rulers were hard-pressed to fight off
the native bands that raided their forts. Here the son of a Colonel
of the Guides, a British regiment, chases the native chieftain Kamal
through a dangerous valley, the Tongue of Jagai. Now discover
what happened when East and West did meet!*

Oh East is East, and West is West, and never the twain shall
    meet,
Till Earth and Sky stand presently at God's great Judgment
    Seat;
But there is neither East nor West, Border, nor Breed, nor
    Birth,
When two strong men stand face to face, tho' they come from
    the ends of the earth!

Kamal is out with twenty men to raise the Border side,   5
And he has lifted the Colonel's mare that is the Colonel's
    pride:
He has lifted her out of the stable-door between the dawn and
    the day,
And turned the calkins upon her feet, and ridden her far
    away.
Then up and spoke the Colonel's son that led a troop of the
    Guides:
" Is there never a man of all my men can say where Kamal
    hides? "   10

Then up and spoke Mohammed Khan, the son of the Ressaldar,

" If ye know the track of the morning-mist, ye know where his
pickets are.

" At dusk he harries the Abazai — at dawn he is into
Bonair,

" But he must go by Fort Bukloh to his own place to fare,

" So if ye gallop to Fort Bukloh as fast as a bird can fly,   15

" By the favor of God ye may cut him off, ere he win to the
Tongue of Jagai,

" But if he be passed the Tongue of Jagai, right swiftly turn
ye then,

" For the length and the breadth of that grisly plain is sown
with Kamal's men.

" There is rock to the left, and rock to the right, and low, lean
thorn between,

" And ye may hear a breech bolt snick where never a man is
seen."   20

The Colonel's son has taken a horse, and a raw rough dun
was he,

With the mouth of a bell and the heart of Hell, and the head
of the gallows-tree.

The Colonel's son to the Fort has won, they bid him stay to
eat —

Who rides at the tail of a Border thief, he sits not long at
his meat.

He's up and away from Fort Bukloh as fast as he can fly,   25

Till he was aware of his father's mare in the gut of the Tongue
of Jagai,

Till he was aware of his father's mare with Kamal upon her
back,

And when he could spy the white of her eye, he made the
   pistol crack.
He has fired once, he has fired twice, but the whistling ball
   went wide.
" Ye shoot like a soldier," Kamal said. " Show now if ye can
   ride."   30
It's up and over the Tongue of Jagai, as blown dust-devils go,
The dun he fled like a stag of ten, but the mare like a barren
   doe.
The dun he leaned against the bit and slugged his head above,
But the red mare played with the snaffle-bars, as a maiden
   plays with a glove.
There was rock to the left and rock to the right, and low lean
   thorn between,   35
And thrice he heard a breech-bolt snick though never a man
   was seen.
They have ridden the low moon out of the sky, their hoofs
   drum up the dawn,
The dun he went like a wounded bull, but the mare like a
   new-roused fawn.
The dun he fell at a water-course — in a woeful heap fell he,
And Kamal has turned the red mare back, and pulled the rider
   free.   40
He has knocked the pistol out of his hand — small room was
   there to strive,
" 'Twas only by favor of mine," quoth he, " ye rode so long
   alive:
" There was not a rock for twenty miles, there was not a clump
   of tree,
" But covered a man of my own men with his rifle cocked on
   his knee.
" If I had raised my bridle-hand, as I have held it low,   45
" The little jackals that flee so fast, were feasting all in a row:

" If I had bowed my head on my breast, as I have held it high,
" The kite that whistles above us now were gorged till she
    could not fly."
Lightly answered the Colonel's son: " Do good to bird and
    beast,
" But count who come for the broken meats before thou
    makest a feast.   50
" If there should follow a thousand swords to carry my bones
    away,
" Belike the price of a jackal's meal were more than a thief
    could pay.
" They will feed their horse on the standing crop, their men
    on the garnered grain,
" The thatch of the byres will serve their fires when all the
    cattle are slain.
" But if thou thinkest the price be fair, — thy brethren wait
    to sup,   55
" The hound is kin to the jackal-spawn, — howl, dog, and call
    them up!
" And if thou thinkest the price be high, in steer and gear and
    stack,
" Give me my father's mare again, and I'll fight my own way
    back! "

Kamal has gripped him by the hand and set him upon his
    feet.
" No talk shall be of dogs," said he, " when wolf and gray
    wolf meet.   60
" May I eat dirt if thou hast hurt of me in deed or breath;
" What dam of lances brought thee forth to jest at the dawn
    with Death? "
Lightly answered the Colonel's son: " I hold by the blood of
    my clan:

"Take up the mare for my father's gift — by God, she has
    carried a man!"

The red mare ran to the Colonel's son, and nuzzled against his
    breast;   65

"We be two strong men," said Kamal then, "but she loveth
    the younger best.

"So she shall go with a lifter's dower, my turquoise-studded
    rein,

"My broidered saddle and saddle-cloth, and silver stirrups
    twain."

The Colonel's son a pistol drew and held it muzzle-end,

"Ye have taken the one from a foe," said he; "will ye take the
    mate from a friend?"   70

"A gift for a gift," said Kamal straight; "a limb for the risk
    of a limb.

"Thy father has sent his son to me, I'll send my son to him!"

With that he whistled his only son, that dropped from a
    mountain-crest —

He trod the ling like a buck in spring, and he looked like a
    lance in rest.

"Now here is thy master," Kamal said, "who leads a troop
    of the Guides,   75

"And thou must ride at his left side as shield on shoulder
    rides.

"Till Death or I cut loose the tie, at camp and board and bed,

"Thy life is his — thy fate is to guard him with thy head.

"So thou must eat the White Queen's meat, and all her·foes
    are thine,

"And thou must harry thy father's hold for the peace of the
    Border-line,   80

"And thou must make a trooper tough and hack thy way to
    power —

" Belike they will raise thee to Ressaldar when I am hanged in
  Peshawur."
They have looked each other between the eyes, and there they
  have found no fault,
They have taken the Oath of the Brother-in-Blood on leavened
  bread and salt;
They have taken the Oath of the Brother-in-Blood on fire and
  fresh-cut sod,   85
On the hilt and the haft of the Khyber knife, and the Won-
  drous Names of God.
The Colonel's son he rides the mare and Kamal's boy the
  dun,
And two have come back to Fort Bukloh where there went
  forth but one.
And when they drew to the Quarter-Guard, full twenty swords
  flew clear —
There was not a man but carried his feud with the blood of
  the mountaineer.   90
" Ha' done! ha' done! " said the Colonel's son, " Put up the
  steel at your sides!
" Last night ye had struck at a Border thief — tonight 'tis a
  man of the Guides! "

*Oh East is East and West is West, and never the twain shall
  meet,*
*Till Earth and Sky stand presently at God's great Judgment
  Seat;*
*But there is neither East nor West, Border, nor Breed, nor
  Birth,*   95
*When two strong men stand face to face, though they come
  from the ends of the earth.*

RUDYARD KIPLING

The Glove and the Lions

King Francis was a hearty king, and loved a royal sport,
And one day, as his lions fought, sat looking on the court.
The nobles filled the benches, with the ladies in their pride,
And 'mongst them sat the Count de Lorge, with one for whom
    he sighed: 4
And truly 'twas a gallant thing to see that crowning show,
Valor and love, and a king above, and the royal beasts below.

Ramped and roared the lions, with horrid laughing jaws;
They bit, they glared, gave blows like beams, a wind went with
    their paws,
With wallowing might and stifled roar they rolled on one
    another,
Till all the pit with sand and mane was in a thunderous
    smother;   10
The bloody foam above the bars came whisking through the
    air;
Said Francis then, " Faith, gentlemen, we're better here than
    there."

De Lorge's love o'erheard the king, a beauteous, lively dame,
With smiling lips and sharp bright eyes, which always seemed
    the same;   14
She thought: " The Count, my lover, is brave as brave can be;
He surely would do wondrous things to show his love of me.
King, ladies, lovers, all look on; the occasion is divine.
I'll drop my glove, to prove his love; great glory will be mine."

She dropped her glove, to prove his love, then looked at him
    and smiled;
He bowed, and in a moment leaped among the lions wild:

The leap was quick, return was quick, he has regained his
    place,   21
Then threw the glove, but not with love, right in the lady's
    face.
"By heaven," said Francis, "rightly done!" and he rose from
    where he sat;
"No love," quoth he, "but vanity, sets love a task like that."

LEIGH HUNT

Lochinvar

*Sir Walter Scott was not only a great storyteller, author of such
novels as* Ivanhoe, Kenilworth, *and* Rob Roy, *but also a poet. In
his long poem* Marmion, *a story of the fighting between Scotch
clans, the story of "Lochinvar" is sung as a dramatic interlude.*

Oh, young Lochinvar is come out of the west:
Through all the wide border his steed was the best;
And save his good broadsword he weapons had none;
He rode all unarmed and he rode all alone.
So faithful in love, and so dauntless in war,   5
There never was knight like the young Lochinvar!

He stayed not for brake, and he stopped not for stone;
He swam the Esk River where ford there was none:
But ere he alighted at Netherby gate,
The bride had consented, the gallant came late;   10
For a laggard in love, and a dastard in war,
Was to wed the fair Ellen of brave Lochinvar.

So boldly he entered the Netherby Hall,
Among bridesmen, and kinsmen, and brothers, and all:
Then spoke the bride's father, his hand on his sword   15
(For the poor craven bridegroom said never a word),
" O come ye in peace here, or come ye in war,
Or to dance at our bridal, young Lord Lochinvar? " —

" I long wooed your daughter, my suit you denied; —
Love swells like the Solway, but ebbs like its tide!   20
And now am I come, with this lost love of mine,
To lead but one measure, drink one cup of wine:
There are maidens in Scotland more lovely by far,
That would gladly be bride to the young Lochinvar."

The bride kissed the goblet; the knight took it up,   25
He quaffed off the wine, and he threw down the cup.
She looked down to blush, and she looked up to sigh,
With a smile on her lips, and a tear in her eye.
He took her soft hand, ere her mother could bar, —
"Now tread we a measure! " said young Lochinvar.   30

So stately his form, and so lovely her face,
That never a hall such a galliard did grace:
While her mother did fret, and her father did fume,
And the bridegroom stood dangling his bonnet and plume;
And the bride-maidens whispered, " 'T were better by far   35
To have matched our fair cousin with young Lochinvar."

One touch to her hand, and one word in her ear,
When they reached the hall-door, and the charger stood near;
So light to the croupe the fair lady he swung,
So light to the saddle before her he sprung!   40
She is won! we are gone, over bank, bush, and scaur;
" They'll have fleet steeds that follow," quoth young Lochin-
     var.

There was mounting 'mong Græmes of the Netherby clan;
Torsters, Fenwicks, and Musgraves, they rode and they ran;
There was racing and chasing on Cannobie Lee,   45
But the lost bride of Netherby ne'er did they see.
So daring in love, and so dauntless in war,
Have ye e'er heard of gallant like young Lochinvar?

WALTER SCOTT

The Fight at the Bridge (from " Horatius ")

*Horatius (or, to give him his full name, Publius Horatius Cocles)
was a beloved Roman hero. With the help of two companions,
Lartius and Herminius, he held a bridge against an invading army,
the Tuscans, while his soldiers destroyed the bridge. After the
bridge was broken down, Horatius, though wounded, leaped into
the river and swam safely to shore. The event was celebrated by
the English essayist and poet, Thomas Babington Macaulay, in his
Lays of Ancient Rome.*

Meanwhile the Tuscan army,
 Right glorious to behold,
Came flashing back the noonday light,
Rank behind rank, like surges bright
 Of a broad sea of gold.   5
Four hundred trumpets sounded
 A peal of warlike glee,
As that great host, with measured tread,
And spears advanced, and ensigns spread,
Rolled slowly toward the bridge's head,   10
 Where stood the dauntless Three.

The Three stood calm and silent
 And looked upon the foes,
And a great shout of laughter
 From all the vanguard rose: 15
And forth three chiefs came spurring
 Before that deep array;
To earth they sprang, their swords they drew,
And lifted high their shields, and flew
 To win the narrow way: 20

Aunus from green Tifernum,
 Lord of the Hill of Vines;
And Seius, whose eight hundred slaves
 Sicken in Ilva's mines;
And Picus, long to Clusium   25
 Vassal in peace and war,
Who led to fight his Umbrian powers
From that gray crag where, girt with towers,
The fortress of Nequinum lowers
 O'er the pale waves of Nar.   30

Stout Lartius hurled down Aunus
   Into the stream beneath:
Herminius struck at Seius,
   And clove him to the teeth:
At Picus brave Horatius   35
   Darted one fiery thrust,
And the proud Umbrian's gilded arms
   Clashed in the bloody dust.

But now no sound of laughter
   Was heard among the foes.   40
A wild and wrathful clamor
   From all the vanguard rose.
Six spears' length from the entrance
   Halted that deep array,
And for a space no man came forth   45
   To win the narrow way.

But hark! the cry is " Astur! "
   And lo! the ranks divide;
And the great Lord of Luna
   Comes with his stately stride.   50
   Upon his ample shoulders
   Clangs loud the fourfold shield,
And in his hand he shakes the brand
   Which none but he can wield.

He smiled on those bold Romans   55
   A smile serene and high;
He eyed the flinching Tuscans,
   And scorn was in his eye.

Quoth he, " The she-wolf's litter
   Stand savagely at bay: 60
But will ye dare to follow,
   If Astur clears the way? "

Then, whirling up his broadsword
   With both hands to the height,
He rushed against Horatius,   65
   And smote with all his might.
With shield and blade Horatius
   Right deftly turned the blow.
The blow, though turned, came yet too nigh;
It missed his helm, but gashed his thigh: 70
The Tuscans raised a joyful cry
   To see the red blood flow.

He reeled, and on Herminius
   He leaned one breathing-space;
Then, like a wild-cat mad with wounds,   75
   Sprang right at Astur's face:
Through teeth and skull and helmet
   So fierce a thrust he sped,
The good sword stood a hand-breadth out
   Behind the Tuscan's head.   80

And the great Lord of Luna
   Fell at that deadly stroke,
As falls on Mount Alvernus
   A thunder-smitten oak.
Far o'er the crashing forest   85
   The giant arms lie spread;
And the pale augurs, muttering low,
   Gaze on the blasted head.

On Astur's throat Horatius
   Right firmly pressed his heel,   90
And thrice and four times tugged amain
   Ere he wrenched out the steel.
" And see," he cried, " the welcome,
   Fair guests, that waits you here!
What noble Lucumo comes next   95
   To taste our Roman cheer? "

But at his haughty challenge
   A sullen murmur ran,
Mingled of wrath and shame and dread,
   Along that glittering van.   100
There lacked not men of prowess,
   Nor men of lordly race;
For all Etruria's noblest
   Were round the fatal place.

But all Etruria's noblest   105
   Felt their hearts sink to see
On the earth the bloody corpses,
   In the path the dauntless Three:
And, from the ghastly entrance
   Where those bold Romans stood,   110
All shrank, like boys who, unaware,
Ranging the woods to start a hare,
Come to the mouth of the dark lair
Where, growling low, a fierce old bear
   Lies amidst bones and blood.   115

Was none who would be foremost
   To lead such dire attack:
But those behind cried " Forward! "
   And those before cried " Back! "

And backward now and forward   120
    Wavers the deep array;
And on the tossing sea of steel
    To and fro the standards reel;
And the victorious trumpet-peal
    Dies fitfully away.

THOMAS BABINGTON MACAULAY

The *Revenge*

*The sea fight which is described in this poem was an actual en-
counter; it took place in 1591, during one of the wars between England and Spain. Sir Richard Grenville took his small ship, the
Revenge, into battle against the* San Philip *and fifty-two other
Spanish men-of-war. In the poem are echoes of Sir Richard's brav-
ery —* "Fight on! Fight on!" *— as well as of his hatred of Spanish
rule. In the second paragraph there is a reference to the Spanish
Inquisition, a court established to punish religious heretics which
turned into an instrument of terror. Tennyson took most of his
facts from Sir Walter Raleigh's* Report of the Truth of the Fight
about the Isles of Azores.

At Flores in the Azores Sir Richard Grenville lay,
And a pinnace, like a fluttered bird, came flying from far away:
" Spanish ships of war at sea! we have sighted fifty-three! "
Then swore Lord Thomas Howard: " 'Fore God I am no
    coward;
But I cannot meet them here, for my ships are out of gear,   5
And the half my men are sick. I must fly, but follow quick.
We are six ships of the line; can we fight with fifty-three? "

Then spoke Sir Richard Grenville; " I know you are no
    coward;
You fly them for a moment to fight with them again.

But I've ninety men and more that are lying sick ashore.   10
I should count myself the coward if I left them, my Lord
    Howard,
To these Inquisition dogs and the devildoms of Spain."

So Lord Howard passed away with five ships of war that day,
Till he melted like a cloud in the silent summer heaven;
But Sir Richard bore in hand all his sick men from the
    land   15
Very carefully and slow,
Men of Bideford in Devon,
And we laid them on the ballast down below;
For we brought them all aboard,
And they blest him in their pain, that they were not left to
    Spain,   20
To the thumbscrew and the stake, for the glory of the Lord.

He had only a hundred seamen to work the ship and to fight,
And he sailed away from Flores till the Spaniard came in sight,
With his huge sea-castles heaving upon the weather bow.
" Shall we fight or shall we fly?   25
Good Sir Richard, tell us now,
For to fight is but to die!
There'll be little of us left by the time this sun be set,"
And Sir Richard said again: " We be all good English men.
Let us bang these dogs of Seville, the children of the devil,   30
For I never turned my back upon Don or devil yet."

Sir Richard spoke and he laughed, and we roared a hurrah,
    and so
The little *Revenge* ran on sheer into the heart of the foe,
With her hundred fighters on deck, and her ninety sick be-
    low;

For half of their fleet to the right and half to the left were
    seen,   35
And the little *Revenge* ran on through the long sea-lane be-
    tween.

Thousands of their soldiers looked down from their decks and
    laughed,
Thousands of their seamen made mock at the mad little craft
Running on and on, till delayed
By their mountainlike *San Philip* that, of fifteen hundred
    tons,   40
And up-shadowing high above us with her yawning tiers of
    guns,
Took the breath from our sails, and we stayed.

And while now the great *San Philip* hung above us like a cloud
Whence the thunderbolt will fall
Long and loud,   45
Four galleons drew away
From the Spanish fleet that day,
And two upon the larboard and two upon the starboard lay,
And the battle-thunder broke from them all.

But anon the great *San Philip*, she bethought herself and
    went   50
Having that within her womb that had left her ill content;
And the rest they came aboard us, and they fought us hand
    to hand,
For a dozen times they came with their pikes and musketeers,
And a dozen times we shook 'em off as a dog that shakes his
    ears
When he leaps from the water to the land.   55

And the sun went down, and the stars came out far over the
    summer sea,

But never a moment ceased the fight of the one and the fifty-
    three.

Ship after ship, the whole night long, their high-built galleons
    came,

Ship after ship, the whole night long, with her battle-thunder
    and flame;

Ship after ship, the whole night long, drew back with her dead
    and her shame.   60

For more were sunk and many were shattered, and so could
    fight us no more —

God of battles, was ever a battle like this in the world before?

For he said " Fight on! fight on! "

Though his vessel was all but a wreck;

And it chanced that, when half of the short summer night was
    gone,   65

With a grisly wound to be dressed he had left the deck,

But a bullet struck him that was dressing it suddenly dead,

And himself he was wounded again in the side and the head,

And he said " Fight on! fight on! "

And the night went down, and the sun smiled out far over the
    summer sea,   70

And the Spanish fleet with broken sides lay round us all in a
    ring;

But they dared not touch us again, for they feared that we still
    could sting,

So they watched what the end would be.

And we had not fought them in vain,

But in perilous plight were we,   75

Seeing forty of our poor hundred were slain,
And half of the rest of us maimed for life
In the crash of the cannonades and the desperate strife;
And the sick men down in the hold were most of them stark
    and cold,
And the pikes were all broken or bent, and the powder was all
    of it spent;   80
And the masts and the rigging were lying over the side;
But Sir Richard cried in his English pride,
" We have fought such a fight for a day and a night
As may never be fought again!
We have won great glory, my men!   85
And a day less or more
At sea or ashore,
We die — does it matter when?
Sink me the ship, Master Gunner — sink her, split her in
    twain!
Fall into the hands of God, not into the hands of Spain! "   90
And the gunner said " Ay, ay," but the seamen made reply:
" We have children, we have wives,
And the Lord hath spared our lives.
We will make the Spaniard promise, if we yield, to let us go;
We shall live to fight again and to strike another blow."   95
And the lion there lay dying, and they yielded to the foe.

And the stately Spanish men to their flagship bore him then,
Where they laid him by the mast, old Sir Richard caught at
    last,
And they praised him to his face with their courtly foreign
    grace;
But he rose upon their decks, and he cried: 100
" I have fought for Queen and Faith like a valiant man and
    true;

I have only done my duty as a man is bound to do:
With a joyful spirit I Sir Richard Grenville die! "
And he fell upon their decks, and he died.

And they stared at the dead that had been so valiant and true,
And had holden the power and glory of Spain so cheap   106
That he dared her with one little ship and his English few;
Was he devil or man? He was devil for aught they knew,
But they sank his body with honor down into the deep,
And they manned the *Revenge* with a swarthier alien
    crew,   110
And away she sailed with her loss and longed for her own;
When a wind from the lands they had ruined awoke from
    sleep,
And the water began to heave and the weather to moan,
And or ever that evening ended a great gale blew,
And a wave like the wave that is raised by an earthquake
    grew,   115
Till it smote on their hulls and their sails and their masts and
    their flags,
And the whole sea plunged and fell on the shot-shattered navy
    of Spain,
And the little *Revenge* herself went down by the island crags
To be lost evermore in the main.

ALFRED TENNYSON

The Charge of the Light Brigade

Here is a stirring description in poetry of an actual battle which took place during the Crimean War between England and Russia. The place was the village of Balaclava near Sevastopol, in southern Russia; the date was October 25, 1854. Due to a blunder, the greatly outnumbered Light Brigade was ordered to charge the en-

tire Russian army. *The Russians were drawn up on both sides of a valley, as well as at the end, and it was literally a " valley of Death . . . the mouth of Hell" to the English soldiers. Of the original six hundred soldiers, less than two hundred came back. It was concerning this charge that the French general, Bosquet, made the famous remark: " It is magnificent; but it is not war."*

Half a league, half a league,
   Half a league onward,
All in the valley of Death
   Rode the six hundred.
" Forward, the Light Brigade!   5
Charge for the guns! " he said:
Into the valley of Death
   Rode the six hundred.

" Forward, the Light Brigade! "
Was there a man dismayed?   10
Not though the soldier knew
   Some one had blundered:
Theirs not to make reply,
Theirs not to reason why,
Theirs but to do and die: 15
Into the valley of Death
   Rode the six hundred.

Cannon to right of them,
Cannon to left of them,
Cannon in front of them   20
   Volleyed and thundered;
Stormed at with shot and shell,
Boldly they rode and well,
Into the jaws of Death,
Into the mouth of Hell   25
   Rode the six hundred.

Flashed all their sabers bare,
Flashed as they turned in air,
Sabering the gunners there,
Charging an army, while   30
    All the world wondered:
Plunged in the battery-smoke
Right through the line they broke;
Cossack and Russian
Reeled from the saber-stroke   35
    Shattered and sundered.
Then they rode back, but not,
    Not the six hundred.

Cannon to right of them,
Cannon to left of them,   40
Cannon behind them
    Volleyed and thundered;
Stormed at with shot and shell,
While horse and hero fell,
They that had fought so well   45
Came through the jaws of Death
Back from the mouth of Hell,
All that was left of them,
    Left of six hundred.

When can their glory fade?   50
O the wild charge they made!
    All the world wondered.
Honor the charge they made!
Honor the Light Brigade,
    Noble six hundred!   55

                        ALFRED TENNYSON

Burial of Sir John Moore

This and the following poem record two incidents in the Napo-leonic wars. The scene of the first poem is Spain, in 1809, and the hero is the English general, Sir John Moore, who was fighting a losing campaign against Napoleon. Moore stayed behind to protect the retreat of his cavalry and artillery at the port of Corunna and lost his life during the action. Even his enemies, the French, were impressed by his heroism and erected a monument in his honor.

The second poem describes a scene near the town of Ratisbon, which the Germans called Regensburg. Napoleon is worried; he stands with head sunk ("prone brow") waiting for news of the outcome of an attack on Ratisbon. It is an anxious moment as the messenger rides through the smoke of battle, bearing the news.

Not a drum was heard, not a funeral note,
　As his corpse to the rampart we hurried;
Not a soldier discharged his farewell shot
　O'er the grave where our hero we buried.

We buried him darkly, at dead of night,　　　　5
　The sods with our bayonets turning;
By the struggling moonbeams' misty light,
　And the lantern dimly burning.

No useless coffin enclosed his breast,
　Not in sheet or in shroud we wound him;　　　10
But he lay, like a warrior taking his rest,
　With his martial cloak around him.

Few and short were the prayers we said,
　And we spoke not a word of sorrow;
But we steadfastly gazed on the face of the dead,　15
　And we bitterly thought of the morrow.

We thought, as we hollowed his narrow bed,
    And smoothed down his lonely pillow,
That the foe and the stranger would tread o'er his head,
    And we far away on the billow!   20

Lightly they'll talk of the spirit that's gone,
    And o'er his cold ashes upbraid him;
But little he'll reck, if they let him sleep on
    In the grave where a Briton has laid him!

But half of our heavy task was done,   25
    When the clock struck the hour for retiring;
And we heard the distant and random gun
    That the foe was suddenly firing.

Slowly and sadly we laid him down,
    From the field of his fame fresh and gory!   30
We carved not a line, and we raised not a stone,
    But we left him alone with his glory.

CHARLES WOLFE

Incident of the French Camp

You know, we French stormed Ratisbon.
    A mile or so away,
On a little mound, Napoleon
    Stood on our storming-day;
With neck out-thrust, you fancy how,   5
    Legs wide, arms locked behind,
As if to balance the prone brow
    Oppressive with its mind.

Just as perhaps he mused " My plans
   That soar, to earth may fall,   10
Let once my army-leader Lannes
   Waver at yonder wall " —
Out 'twixt the battery smokes there flew
   A rider, bound on bound
Full-galloping; nor bridle drew   15
   Until he reached the mound.

Then off there flung in smiling joy,
   And held himself erect
By just his horse's mane, a boy:
   You hardly could suspect —   20
(So tight he kept his lips compressed,
   Scarce any blood came through)
You looked twice ere you saw his breast
   Was all but shot in two.

" Well," cried he, " Emperor, by God's grace   25
   We've got you Ratisbon!
The Marshal's in the market place,
   And you'll be there anon
To see your flag-bird flap his vans
   Where I, to heart's desire,   30
Perched him! " The chief's eye flashed; his plans
   Soared up again like fire.

The chief's eye flashed; but presently
   Softened itself, as sheathes
A film the mother-eagle's eye   35
   When her bruised eaglet breathes;
" You're wounded! " " Nay," the soldier's pride
   Touched to the quick, he said:

"I'm killed, Sire!" And, his chief beside,
   Smiling, the boy fell dead.

ROBERT BROWNING

Dunkirk

Things looked bad for the friends of democracy in 1940. The German armies had conquered Poland, overrun Denmark and Norway, and had forced Holland and Belgium to surrender. Pushing into France, they threatened to drive the British armies into the sea. On June 28, 1940, the British started evacuating men from the port of Dunkirk. The evacuation lasted five days; the troops had to cross the beaches under fire of Nazi guns and aircraft. More than a quarter of a million men would have been lost had not boats of all kinds — yachts, fishing schooners, excursion boats, little pleasure craft — put out from England to come to the rescue. Across the open waters came anything that could float, unprotected and uncommanded, fired on without being able to strike back, their one object being to reach Dunkirk and bring back the trapped soldiers.

Will came back from school that day,
And he had little to say.
But he stood a long time looking down
To where the gray-green Channel water
Slapped at the foot of the little town,   5
And to where his boat, the *Sarah P*,
Bobbed at the tide on an even keel,
With her one old sail, patched at the leech,
Furled like a slattern down at heel.

He stood for a while above the beach;   10
He saw how the wind and current caught her.
He looked a long time out to sea.

There was steady wind and the sky was pale,
And a haze in the east that looked like smoke.

Will went back to the house to dress.   15
He was halfway through when his sister Bess,
Who was near fourteen and younger than he
By just two years, came home from play.
She asked him, " Where are you going, Will? "
He said, " For a good long sail."   20
" Can I come along? "
                        " No, Bess," he spoke.
" I may be gone for a night and a day."
Bess looked at him. She kept very still.
She had heard the news of the Flanders rout,
How the English were trapped above Dunkirk,   25
And the fleet had gone to get them out —
But everyone thought that it wouldn't work.
There was too much fear, there was too much doubt.

She looked at him and he looked at her.
They were English children, born and bred.   30
He frowned her down, but she wouldn't stir.
She shook her proud young head.
" You'll need a crew," she said.

They raised the sail on the *Sarah P*,
Like a penoncel on a young knight's lance,   35
And headed the *Sarah* out to sea,
To bring their soldiers home from France.

There was no command, there was no set plan,
But six hundred boats went out with them
On the gray-green waters, sailing fast,   40
River excursion and fisherman,

Tug and schooner and racing M,
And the little boats came following last.

From every harbor and town they went
Who had sailed their craft in the sun and rain,   45
From the South Downs, from the cliffs of Kent,
From the village street, from the country lane.
There are twenty miles of rolling sea
From coast to coast, by the seagull's flight,
But the tides were fair and the wind was free,   50
And they raised Dunkirk by the fall of night.

They raised Dunkirk with its harbor torn
By the blasted stern and the sunken prow;
They had raced for fun on an English tide,
They were English children bred and born,   55
And whether they lived or whether they died,
They raced for England now.

Bess was as white as the *Sarah's* sail,
She set her teeth and smiled at Will.
He held his course for the smoky veil   60
Where the harbor narrowed thin and long.
The British ships were firing strong.

He took the *Sarah* into his hands,
He drove her in through fire and death
To the wet men waiting on the sands.   65
He got his load and he got his breath,
And she came about, and the wind fought her.
He shut his eyes and he tried to pray.
He saw his England where she lay,
The wind's green home, the sea's proud daughter,   70

Still in the moonlight, dreaming deep,
The English cliffs and the English loam —
He had fourteen men to get away,
And the moon was clear and the night like day
For planes to see where the white sails creep   75
Over the black water.

He closed his eyes and he prayed for her;
He prayed to the men who had made her great,
Who had built her land of forest and park,
Who had made the seas an English lake;   80
He prayed for a fog to bring the dark;
He prayed to get home for England's sake.
And the fog came down on the rolling sea,
And covered the ships with English mist.
The diving planes were baffled and blind.   85

For Nelson was there in the *Victory*,
With his one good eye, and his sullen twist,
And guns were out on *The Golden Hind*,
Their shot flashed over the *Sarah P*.
He could hear them cheer as he came about.   90

By burning wharves, by battered slips,
Galleon, frigate, and brigantine,
The old dead Captains fought their ships,
And the great dead Admirals led the line.
It was England's night, it was England's sea.   95

The fog rolled over the harbor key.
Bess held to the stays and conned him out.

And all through the dark, while the *Sarah's* wake
Hissed behind him, and vanished in foam,
There at his side sat Francis Drake,   100
And held him true and steered him home.

                                        ROBERT   NATHAN

3
UNFORGETTABLE
PEOPLE

Miniver Cheevy

Miniver Cheevy, child of scorn,
　Grew lean while he assailed the seasons;
He wept that he was ever born,
　And he had reasons.

Miniver loved the days of old　　　　　　　　　　5
　When swords were bright and steeds were prancing;
The vision of a warrior bold
　Would set him dancing.

Miniver sighed for what was not,
　And dreamed, and rested from his labors;　　　　10
He dreamed of Thebes and Camelot,
　And Priam's neighbors.

Miniver mourned the ripe renown
　That made so many a name so fragrant;
He mourned Romance, now on the town,　　　　　15
　And Art, a vagrant.

Miniver loved the Medici,
　Albeit he had never seen one;
He would have sinned incessantly
　Could he have been one.　　　　　　　　　　　20

Miniver cursed the commonplace
   And eyed a khaki suit with loathing;
He missed the medieval grace
   Of iron clothing.

Miniver scorned the gold he sought,   25
   But sore annoyed was he without it;
Miniver thought, and thought, and thought,
   And thought about it.

Miniver Cheevy, born too late,
   Scratched his head and kept on thinking;   30
Miniver coughed, and called it fate,
   And kept on drinking.

EDWIN ARLINGTON ROBINSON

Annabel Lee

It was many and many a year ago,
   In a kingdom by the sea,
That a maiden there lived whom you may know
   By the name of Annabel Lee;
And this maiden she lived with no other thought   5
   Than to love and be loved by me.

I was a child and *she* was a child,
   In this kingdom by the sea:
But we loved with a love that was more than love —
   I and my Annabel Lee;
                                  10
With a love that the wingèd seraphs of heaven
   Coveted her and me.

And this was the reason that, long ago,
   In this kingdom by the sea,
A wind blew out of a cloud, chilling   15
   My beautiful Annabel Lee;
So that her highborn kinsmen came
   And bore her away from me,
To shut her up in a sepulcher
   In this kingdom by the sea.   20

The angels, not half so happy in heaven,
   Went envying her and me —
Yes! — that was the reason (as all men know,
   In this kingdom by the sea)
That the wind came out of the cloud by night,   25
   Chilling and killing my Annabel Lee.

But our love it was stronger by far than the love
   Of those who were older than we —
   Of many far wiser than we —
And neither the angels in heaven above,   30
   Nor the demons down under the sea,
Can ever dissever my soul from the soul
   Of the beautiful Annabel Lee:

For the moon never beams, without bringing me dreams
   Of the beautiful Annabel Lee;   35
And the stars never rise, but I feel the bright eyes
   Of the beautiful Annabel Lee;
And so, all the night-tide, I lie down by the side
Of my darling, — my darling, — my life and my bride,
   In her sepulcher there by the sea,   40
   In her tomb by the side of the sea.

                                EDGAR ALLAN POE

Three Canterbury Pilgrims

Poetry is often concerned with the portrayal of people; and it is safe to say that some of the greatest poetry displays the greatest portraits. Chaucer and Shakespeare created ever-living characters; their looks, their actions, and their very nature are drawn for us unforgettably in a few lines. These three portraits are from Chaucer's Canterbury Tales, *translated into modern English by the editor. In the Prologue of his long poem, Chaucer describes the various men and women who go on a religious pilgrimage to the town of Canterbury. They are typical figures of the Middle Ages.*

A Knight

A Knight there was, and that a worthy man,
Who, from the moment when he first began
To ride forth, loved the code of chivalry:
Honor and truth, freedom and courtesy.
His lord's war had established him in worth;   5
He rode — and no man further — ends of earth
In heathen parts as well as Christendom,
Honored wherever he might go or come . . .
Of mortal battles he had seen fifteen,
And fought hard for our faith at Tramassene   10
Thrice in the lists, and always slain his foe.
This noble knight was even led to go
To Turkey were he fought most valiantly
Against the heathen hordes for Palaty.
Renowned he was; and, worthy, he was wise —   15
Prudence, with him, was more than mere disguise.
He was as meek in manner as a maid.
Vileness he shunned, rudeness he never said
In all his life, respecting each man's right.
He was a truly perfect, noble knight.   20

Amor Vincit Omnia

A Squire

With him there was his son, a youthful Squire
A merry blade, a lover full of fire;
With locks as curled as though laid in a press —
Scarce twenty years of age was he, I guess.
In stature he was of an average length,   25
Wondrously active, bright, and great in strength.
He proved himself a soldier handsomely
In Flanders, in Artois and Picardy,
Bearing himself so well, in so short space,
Hoping to stand high in his lady's grace.   30
Embroidered was his clothing, like a mead
Full of fresh flowers, shining white and red.
Singing he was, or fluting, all the day —
He was as fresh as is the month of May.
Short was his gown; his sleeves were long and wide;   35
Well did he sit his horse, and nimbly ride,
He could make songs, intune them or indite,
Joust, play and dance, and also draw and write.
So well could he repeat love's endless tale,
He slept no more than does the nightingale.   40
Yet he was humble, courteous and able,
And carved before his father when at table.

A Prioress

There also was a nun, a Prioress
Whose smile was simple. Quiet, even coy,
The worst oath that she swore was " By Saint Loy! "   45
And she was known as Sister Eglantine.
Sweetly she sang the services divine,
Intoning through her nose the melody.
Fairly she spoke her French, and skilfully,

After the school of Stratford-at-the-Bow —   50
Parisian French was not for her to know.
Precise at table and well-bred withal
Her lips would never let a morsel fall;
She never wet her fingers in her sauce,
But carried every tidbit without loss   55
Of even the smallest drop upon her breast.
Manners and good behavior pleased her best.
She always wiped her upper lip so clean
That not a speck of grease was ever seen
Upon the cup from which she drank. Her food   60
Was reached for neatly; she was never rude.
Though her demeanor was the very best,
Her mood was amiable, she loved a jest;
She always tried to copy each report
Of how the latest fashion ran at court,   65
And yet to hold herself with dignity.
But, speaking of her inner nature, she
Was so devout, so full of sympathy,
She would lament if she would have to see
A mouse caught in a trap, if it had bled.   70
A few small dogs she had, and these she fed
With roasted meat, or milk and sweetened bread,
And wept aloud if one of them were dead,
Or if a person struck and made them smart —
She was all goodness and a tender heart.   75
Her wimple draped itself a modest way;
Her nose was straight, her eyes transparent gray,
Her mouth was small, but very soft and red,
Hers was a noble and a fair forehead,
Almost a span in breadth, one realized;   80
For she was small but scarcely undersized.
Her cloak was well designed, I was aware;

Her arm was graced with corals, and she bare
A string in which the green glass beads were bold,
And from it hung a brilliant brooch of gold   85
On which there was engraved a large, crowned A,
Followed by *Amor vincit omnia.*

GEOFFREY CHAUCER
Modern Version by Louis Untermeyer

A Shakespeare Gallery

*In Shakespeare the colorfulness of verse and dramatic power com-
bine to create magnificent pictures of men and women — their
hopes, their actions, their destinies. The first two sketches that follow are from* Julius Caesar. *In the first, Cassius gives us an angry
view of a dictator, the great Caesar; in the second, we hear the
speech made on the death of Brutus, who joined in the assassination
of Caesar and met death on the battlefield. Then follow lyrical pictures of two heroines:* Juliet, *young and gentle, and* Cleopatra,
*proud and beautiful. Next, there is a portrait of Hamlet drawn by
his forsaken sweetheart, Ophelia. In order to trap his murderous
uncle, Hamlet pretends to be mad and goes raving before Ophelia,
who is grief-stricken when she thinks his " noble mind is . . .
o'erthrown." Finally, there is a fanciful sketch of Queen Mab,
queen of the Fairies. This speech is said humorously by Mercutio
in* Romeo and Juliet *and has always been a favorite of actors because of its fancy foolishness.*

Caesar

Why, man, he doth bestride the narrow world
Like a Colossus, and we petty men
Walk under his huge legs and peep about
To find ourselves dishonorable graves.
Men at some time are masters of their fates: 5
The fault, dear Brutus, is not in our stars,

But in ourselves, that we are underlings.
Brutus, and Caesar: what should be in that Caesar?
Why should that name be sounded more than yours?
Write them together, yours is as fair a name;   10
Sound them, it doth become the mouth as well;
Weigh them, it is as heavy; conjure with 'em,
Brutus will start a spirit as soon as Caesar.
Now, in the names of all the gods at once,
Upon what meat doth this our Caesar feed,   15
That he is grown so great? Age, thou art shamed!
Rome, thou hast lost the breed of noble bloods!
When went there by an age, since the great flood,
But it was famed with more than with one man?
When could they say till now that talked of Rome   20
That her wide walls encompassed but one man?
Now is it Rome indeed, and room enough,
When there is in it but one only man.

(From Julius Caesar. Act I; scene 2)

Brutus

This was the noblest Roman of them all:
All the conspirators, save only he,   25
Did that they did in envy of great Caesar;
He only, in a general honest thought
And common good to all, made one of them.
His life was gentle, and the elements
So mixed in him that Nature might stand up   30
And say to all the world " This was a man! "

(From Julius Caesar. Act V; scene 5)

Juliet

Soft! what light through yonder window breaks?
It is the east, and Juliet is the sun!
Arise, fair sun, and kill the envious moon,

Who is already sick and pale with grief,   35
That thou her maid are far more fair than she:
Be not her maid, since she is envious;

Her vestal livery is but sick and green,
And none but fools do wear it; cast it off.
It is my lady; O, it is my love!   40
O, that she knew she were!
She speaks, yet she says nothing: what of that?
Her eye discourses, I will answer it.
I am too bold, 'tis not to me she speaks:
Two of the fairest stars in all the heaven,   45
Having some business, do intreat her eyes

To twinkle in their spheres till they return.
What if her eyes were there, they in her head?
The brightness of her cheek would shame those stars
As daylight doth a lamp; her eyes in heaven   50
Would through the airy region stream so bright
That birds would sing and think it were not night.
See, how she leans her cheek upon her hand!
O, that I were a glove upon that hand,
That I might touch that cheek!   55

(From Romeo and Juliet. Act II; scene 2)

Cleopatra

Age cannot wither her, nor custom stale
Her infinite variety. Other women cloy
The appetites they feed, but she makes hungry
Where most she satisfies. . . .

               And Antony,
Enthroned i' the market place, did sit alone,   60
Whistling to the air; which, but for vacancy,
Had gone to gaze on Cleopatra too,
And made a gap in nature.

(From Antony and Cleopatra. Act II; scene 2)

Hamlet

O, what a noble mind is here o'erthrown!
The courtier's, soldier's, scholar's, eye, tongue, sword: 65
The expectancy and rose of the fair state,
The glass of fashion and the mold of form,
The observed of all observers, quite, quite down!
And I, of ladies most deject and wretched,
That sucked the honey of his music vows,   70
Now see that noble and most sovereign reason,
Like sweet bells jangled, out of tune and harsh;

That unmatched form and feature of blown youth
Blasted with ecstasy. O, woe is me,
To have seen what I have seen, see what I see!   75

(From *Hamlet*. Act III; scene 1)

Queen Mab

She is the fairies' midwife, and she comes
In shape no bigger than an agate-stone
On the forefinger of an alderman,
Drawn with a team of little atomies
Athwart men's noses as they lie asleep: 80
Her wagon-spokes made of long spinners' legs;
The cover, of the wings of grasshoppers;
Her traces, of the smallest spider's web;
Her collars, of the moonshine's watery beams;
Her whip, of cricket's bones; the lash, of film;   85
Her wagoner, a small gray-coated gnat,
Not half so big as a round little worm
Pricked from the lazy finger of a maid:
Her chariot is an empty hazel nut,
Made by the joiner squirrel or old grub,   90
Time out o' mind the fairies' coachmakers.
And in this state she gallops night by night
Through lovers' brains, and then they dream of love;
O'er courtiers' knees, that dream on court'sies straight;
O'er lawyers' fingers, who straight dream on fees;   95
O'er ladies' lips, who straight on kisses dream,
Which oft the angry Mab with blisters plagues,
Because their breaths with sweetmeats tainted are:
Sometimes she gallops o'er a courtier's nose,
And then dreams he of smelling out a suit;   100
And sometime comes she with a tithe-pig's tail
Tickling a parson's nose as he lies asleep,

Then dreams he of another benefice:
Sometime she driveth o'er a soldier's neck,
And then dreams he of cutting foreign throats,   105
Of breaches, ambuscadoes, Spanish blades;

Of healths five fathom deep; and then anon
Drums in his ear, at which he starts and wakes,
And being thus frighted swears a prayer or two,
And sleeps again. This is that very Mab   110
That plats the manes of horses in the night,
And bakes the elf-lock in foul sluttish hairs,
Which once untangled much misfortune bodes.
This is she —   (From *Romeo and Juliet*. Act I; scene 4)

WILLIAM SHAKESPEARE

The Death of the Hired Man

This quiet but dramatic poem is a study of three characters: a New England farmer, his tender-hearted wife, and a hired hand who, though old and shiftless, is still proud. The three people involved are wonderfully revealed through a conversation in ordinary, everyday speech — and the person of whom we learn most is the one who never appears.

Mary sat musing on the lamp-flame at the table
Waiting for Warren. When she heard his step,
She ran on tip-toe down the darkened passage
To meet him in the doorway with the news
And put him on his guard. " Silas is back."   5
She pushed him outward with her through the door
And shut it after her. " Be kind," she said.
She took the market things from Warren's arms
And set them on the porch, then drew him down
To sit beside her on the wooden steps.   10

" When was I ever anything but kind to him?
But I'll not have the fellow back," he said.
" I told him so last haying, didn't I?
' If he left then,' I said, ' that ended it.'
What good is he? Who else will harbor him   15
At his age for the little he can do?
What help he is there's no depending on.
Off he goes always when I need him most.
' He thinks he ought to earn a little pay,
Enough at least to buy tobacco with,   20
So he won't have to beg and be beholden.'
' All right,' I say, ' I can't afford to pay
Any fixed wages, though I wish I could.'

' Someone else can.' ' Then someone else will have to.'
I shouldn't mind his bettering himself   25
If that was what it was. You can be certain,
When he begins like that, there's someone at him
Trying to coax him off with pocket-money, —
In haying time, when any help is scarce.
In winter he comes back to us. I'm done."   30

" Sh! not so loud: he'll hear you," Mary said.

" I want him to: he'll have to soon or late."

" He's worn out. He's asleep beside the stove.
When I came up from Rowe's I found him here,
Huddled against the barn-door fast asleep,   35
A miserable sight, and frightening, too —
You needn't smile — I didn't recognize him —
I wasn't looking for him — and he's changed.
Wait till you see."

        " Where did you say he'd been? "

" He didn't say. I dragged him to the house,   40
And gave him tea and tried to make him smoke.
I tried to make him talk about his travels.
Nothing would do: he just kept nodding off."

" What did he say? Did he say anything? "

" But little."

        " Anything? Mary, confess   45
He said he'd come to ditch the meadow for me."

" Warren! "

"But did he? I just want to know."

"Of course he did. What would you have him say?
Surely you wouldn't grudge the poor old man
Some humble way to save his self-respect.   50
He added, if you really care to know,
He meant to clear the upper pasture, too.
That sounds like something you have heard before?
Warren, I wish you could have heard the way
He jumbled everything. I stopped to look   55
Two or three times — he made me feel so queer —
To see if he was talking in his sleep.
He ran on Harold Wilson — you remember —
The boy you had in haying four years since.
He's finished school, and teaching in his college.   60
Silas declares you'll have to get him back.
He says they two will make a team for work:
Between them they will lay this farm as smooth!
The way he mixed that in with other things.
He thinks young Wilson a likely lad, though daft   65
On education — you know how they fought
All through July under the blazing sun,
Silas up on the cart to build the load,
Harold along beside to pitch it on."

"Yes, I took care to keep well out of earshot."   70

"Well, those days trouble Silas like a dream.
You wouldn't think they would. How some things linger!
Harold's young college boy's assurance piqued him.
After so many years he still keeps finding
Good arguments he sees he might have used.   75
I sympathize. I know just how it feels

To think of the right thing to say too late.
Harold's associated in his mind with Latin.
He asked me what I thought of Harold's saying
He studied Latin like the violin   80
Because he liked it — that an argument!
He said he couldn't make the boy believe
He could find water with a hazel prong —
Which showed how much good school had ever done him.
He wanted to go over that. But most of all   85
He thinks if he could have another chance
To teach him how to build a load of hay — "

" I know, that's Silas' one accomplishment.
He bundles every forkful in its place,
And tags and numbers it for future reference,   90
So he can find and easily dislodge it
In the unloading. Silas does that well.
He takes it out in bunches like big birds' nests.
You never see him standing on the hay
He's trying to lift, straining to lift himself."   95

" He thinks if he could teach him that, he'd be
Some good perhaps to someone in the world.
He hates to see a boy the fool of books.
Poor Silas, so concerned for other folk,
And nothing to look backward to with pride,   100
And nothing to look forward to with hope,
So now and never any different."

Part of a moon was falling down the west,
Dragging the whole sky with it to the hills.
Its light poured softly in her lap. She saw it   105
And spread her apron to it. She put out her hand

Among the harp-like morning-glory strings,
Taut with the dew from garden bed to eaves,
As if she played unheard some tenderness
That wrought on him beside her in the night.   110
"Warren," she said, "he has come home to die:
You needn't be afraid he'll leave you this time."

"Home," he mocked gently.

                              "Yes, what else but home?
It all depends on what you mean by home.
Of course he's nothing to us, any more   115
Than was the hound that came a stranger to us
Out of the woods, worn out upon the trail."

"Home is the place where, when you have to go there,
They have to take you in."

                              "I should have called it
Something you somehow haven't to deserve."   120

Warren leaned out and took a step or two,
Picked up a little stick, and brought it back
And broke it in his hand and tossed it by.
"Silas has better claim on us you think
Than on his brother? Thirteen little miles   125
As the road winds would bring him to his door.
Silas has walked that far no doubt today.
Why didn't he go there? His brother's rich,
A somebody — director in the bank."

"He never told us that."

                              "We know it though."   130

" I think his brother ought to help, of course.
I'll see to that if there is need. He ought of right
To take him in, and might be willing to —
He may be better than appearances.
But have some pity on Silas. Do you think   135
If he had any pride in claiming kin
Or anything he looked for from his brother,
He'd keep so still about him all this time? "

" I wonder what's between them."

                                    " I can tell you.
Silas is what he is — we wouldn't mind him —   140
But just the kind that kinsfolk can't abide.
He never did a thing so very bad.
He don't know why he isn't quite as good
As anybody. Worthless though he is,
He won't be made ashamed to please his brother."   145

" *I* can't think Si ever hurt anyone."

" No, but he hurt my heart the way he lay
And rolled his old head on that sharp-edged chair-back
He wouldn't let me put him on the lounge.
You must go in and see what you can do.   150
I made the bed up for him there tonight.
You'll be surprised at him — how much he's broken.
His working days are done; I'm sure of it."

" I'd not be in a hurry to say that."

" I haven't been. Go, look, see for yourself.   155
But, Warren, please remember how it is:
He's come to help you ditch the meadow.
He has a plan. You mustn't laugh at him.

He may not speak of it, and then he may.
I'll sit and see if that small sailing cloud   160
Will hit or miss the moon."

                         It hit the moon.
Then there were three there, making a dim row,
The moon, the little silver cloud, and she.

Warren returned — too soon, it seemed to her,
Slipped to her side, caught up her hand and waited.   165

" Warren? " she questioned.

                         " Dead," was all he answered.

                                        ROBERT FROST

To an Athlete Dying Young

The time you won your town the race
We chaired you through the market place;
Man and boy stood cheering by,
And home we brought you shoulder-high.

Today, the road all runners come,   5
Shoulder-high we bring you home,
And set you at your threshold down,
Townsman of a stiller town.

Smart lad, to slip betimes away
From fields where glory does not stay,   10
And early though the laurel grows
It withers quicker than the rose.

Eyes the shady night has shut
Cannot see the record cut,

And silence sounds no worse than cheers   15
After earth has stopped the ears:

Now you will not swell the rout
Of lads that wore their honors out,
Runners whom renown outran
And the name died before the man.   20

So set, before its echoes fade,
The fleet foot on the sill of shade,
And hold to the low lintel up
The still-defended challenge-cup.

And round that early-laureled head   25
Will flock to gaze the strengthless dead,
And find unwithered on its curls
The garland briefer than a girl's.

A. E. HOUSMAN

Achilles Deatheridge

The title of this poem is misleading to some extent. It is the name of a young Union soldier who is questioned about a mistake he made while standing guard. The important person is a plain figure, almost like a " sooty cannoneer."

" Your name is Achilles Deatheridge?
    How old are you, my boy? "
" I'm sixteen past, and I went to the war
    From Athens, Illinois."

" Achilles Deatheridge, you have done   5
    A deed of dreadful note."

" It comes of his wearing a battered hat,
    And a rusty, wrinkled coat."

" Why, didn't you know how plain he is?
    And didn't you ever hear   10
That he goes through the lines by day or night
    Like a sooty cannoneer? "

" You must have been half dead for sleep,
    For the dawn was growing bright."
" Well, Captain, I had stood right there   15
    Since six o'clock last night.

" I cocked my gun at the swish of the grass,
    And how am I at fault
When a dangerous looking man won't stop
    When a sentry hollers halt?   20

" I cried out halt, and he only smiled
    And waved his hand like that.
Why, any Johnnie could wear the coat
    And any fellow the hat.

" I hollered halt again, and he stopped   25
    And lighted a fresh cigar.
I never noticed his shoulder badge,
    And I never noticed a star."

" So you arrested him? Well, Achilles,
    When you hear the swish of the grass,   30
If it's General Grant inspecting the lines,
    Hereafter let him pass."

                        EDGAR LEE MASTERS

High Flight

John Gillespie Magee, Jr., was born in Shanghai, the son of two American missionaries. He did not come to the United States until 1939, at which time he gave up a scholarship at Yale in order to enlist in the Royal Canadian Air Force. For a little more than a year he flew with a Spitfire Squadron, but was shot down on December 11, 1941. He was just nineteen years old. His sonnet, " High Flight," was composed a year before his death, after his first flight into the stratosphere, and has become one of the most quoted poems of World War II.

Oh, I have slipped the surly bonds of earth,
And danced the skies on laughter-silvered wings;
Sunward I've climbed and joined the tumbling mirth
Of sun-split clouds — and done a hundred things
You have not dreamed of — wheeled and soared and swung
High in the sunlit silence. Hovering there
I've chased the shouting wind along and flung
My eager craft through footless halls of air.
Up, up the long delirious burning blue
I've topped the windswept heights with easy grace,
Where never lark, or even eagle, flew;
And, while with silent, lifting mind I've trod
The high untrespassed sanctity of space,
Put out my hand, and touched the face of God.

JOHN GILLESPIE MAGEE, JR.

The Soldier

If I should die, think only this of me;
    That there's some corner of a foreign field
That is for ever England. There shall be
    In that rich earth a richer dust concealed;
A dust whom England bore, shaped, made aware,
    Gave, once, her flowers to love, her ways to roam,
A body of England's breathing English air,
    Washed by the rivers, blest by suns of home.

And think, this heart, all evil shed away,
    A pulse in the eternal mind, no less
        Gives somewhere back the thoughts by England given;
Her sights and sounds; dreams happy as her day;

And laughter, learned of friends; and gentleness,
In hearts at peace, under an English heaven.

RUPERT BROOKE

The Cowboy

He wears a big hat, big spurs, and all that,
    And leggings of fancy fringed leather;
He takes pride in his boots and the pistol he shoots,
    And he's happy in all kinds of weather.

He's fond of his horse — it's a broncho, of course —   5
    And oh, he can ride like the devil.
He is old for his years, and he always appears
    Like a fellow who's lived on the level.

He can sing, he can cook, yet his eyes have the look
    Of a man that to fear is a stranger;   10
Yes, his cool, quiet nerve is ready to serve
    For a life full of duty and danger.

He gets little to eat and he's quick on his feet,
    And for fashion — oh, well, he's not in it.
He can rope a gay steer when it gets on his ear   15
    At the rate of two-forty a minute.

His saddle's the best in the wild, woolly West
    (Sometimes it will cost sixty dollars),
Ah, he knows all the tricks when he brands mavericks,
    And his knowledge is not got from scholars.   20

He is loyal as steel, but demands a square deal,
    And he hates and despises a coward.
Yet the cowboy, you'll find, to women is kind —
    And he'll fight till by death overpowered.

AUTHOR UNKNOWN

The Prisoner of Chillon

*François Bonnivard, the hero of this tale, was an actual person, a
Swiss priest and politician who was born in 1496. He conspired
with other patriots to rebel against the Duke of Savoy, who con-
trolled the country, and to establish a free republic. He was captured and twice imprisoned; the second time he was held for seven
years in the dark castle of Chillon, which was built on a rock off
the shore of Lake Geneva, sometimes called Lake Leman.*

*In 1816, the English poet, Byron, visited the castle and its under-
ground dungeons. There he wrote the moving monologue, "The
Prisoner of Chillon." Byron elaborated upon the original story. He
made Bonnivard one of six brothers, all of whom were punished
for their convictions. In Byron's poem the father and two sons die
on the battlefield; one son is burned at the stake; and three are
thrown into the castle dungeon. Much of the poem is invented,
but the details are graphic and the surrounding Alpine landscape
is accurately described. In Bonnivard, Bryon symbolizes all those
who suffer in the cause of humanity.*

My hair is gray, but not with years,
    Nor grew it white
    In a single night,
As men's have grown from sudden fears;
My limbs are bowed, though not with toil,   5
    But rusted with a vile repose,
For they have been a dungeon's spoil,
    And mine has been the fate of those
To whom the goodly earth and air
Are banned, and barred — forbidden fare;   10
But this was for my father's faith
I suffered chains and courted death;
That father perished at the stake
For tenets he would not forsake;
And for the same his lineal race   15
In darkness found a dwelling-place;
We were seven — who now are one,
    Six in youth, and one in age,
Finished as they had begun,
Proud of Persecution's rage;   20
One in fire, and two in field
Their belief with blood have sealed,
Dying as their father died,
For the God their foes denied;
Three were in a dungeon cast,   25
Of whom this wreck is left the last.
There are seven pillars of Gothic mold,
In Chillon's dungeons deep and old,
There are seven columns, massy and gray,
Dim with a dull imprisoned ray,   30
A sunbeam which hath lost its way
And through the crevice and the cleft
Of the thick wall is fallen and left;

Creeping o'er the floor so damp,
Like a marsh's meteor lamp.   35
And in each pillar there is a ring,
    And in each ring there is a chain;
That iron is a cankering thing,
    For in these limbs its teeth remain,
With marks that will not wear away,   40
Till I have done with this new day,
Which now is painful to these eyes,
Which have not seen the sun to rise
For years — I cannot count them o'er,
I lost their long and heavy score   45
When my last brother drooped and died,
And I lay living by his side.

They chained us each to a column stone,
And we were three — yet, each alone.
We could not move a single pace,   50
We could not see each other's face,
But with that pale and livid light
That made us strangers in our sight.
And thus together — yet apart,
Fettered in hand, but joined in heart,   55
'Twas still some solace, in the dearth
Of the pure elements of earth,
To hearken to each other's speech,
And each turn comforter to each
With some new hope, or legend old,   60
Or song heroically bold;
But even these at length grew cold.
Our voices took a dreary tone,
An echo of the dungeon stone,
    A grating sound, not full and free,   .   65

As they of yore were wont to be;
　　It might be fancy, but to me
They never sounded like our own.

I was the eldest of the three,
　　And to uphold and cheer the rest　　70
　　I ought to do — and did my best —
And each did well in his degree.
　　The youngest, whom my father loved,
Because our mother's brow was given
To him, with eyes as blue as heaven —　　75
　　For him my soul was sorely moved;
And truly might it be distressed
To see such bird in such a nest;
For he was beautiful as day —
　　When day was beautiful to me　　80
　　As to young eagles, being free —
　　A polar day, which will not see
A sunset till its summer's gone,
　　Its sleepless summer of long light,
The snow-clad offspring of the sun;　　85
　　And thus he was as pure and bright,
And in his natural spirit gay,
With tears for naught but others' ills,
And then they flowed like mountain rills,
Unless he could assuage the woe　　90
Which he abhorred to view below.

The other was as pure of mind,
But formed to combat with his kind;
Strong in his frame, and of a mood
Which 'gainst the world in war had stood　　95
And perished in the foremost rank

With joy — but not in chains to pine;
His spirit withered with their clank;
 I saw it silently decline —
 And so perchance in sooth did mine; 100
But yet I forced it on to cheer
Those relics of a home so dear.
He was a hunter of the hills,
 Had followed there the deer and wolf;
 To him this dungeon was a gulf, 105
And fettered feet the worst of ills.

Lake Leman lies by Chillon's walls;
A thousand feet in depth below
Its massy waters meet and flow;
Thus much the fathom-line was sent 110
From Chillon's snow-white battlement,
 Which round about the wave enthralls;
A double dungeon wall and wave
Have made — and like a living grave,
Below the surface of the lake 115
The dark vault lies wherein we lay;
We heard it ripple night and day;
 Sounding o'er our heads it knocked;
And I have felt the winter's spray
Wash through the bars when winds were high 120
And wanton in the happy sky;
 And then the very rock hath rocked,
 And I have felt it shake, unshocked,
Because I could have smiled to see
The death that would have set me free. 125

I said my nearer brother pined,
I said his mighty heart declined,

He loathed and put away his food;
It was not that 'twas coarse and rude,
For we were used to hunter's fare,   130
And for the like had little care.
The milk drawn from the mountain goat
Was changed for water from the moat;
Our bread was such as captives' tears
Have moistened many a thousand years,   135
Since man first pent his fellow men
Like brutes within an iron den;
But what were these to us or him?
These wasted not his heart or limb;
My brother's soul was of that mold   140
Which in a palace had grown cold,
Had his free breathing been denied
The range of the steep mountain's side;
But why delay the truth? — he died.
I saw, and could not hold his head,   145
Nor reach his dying hand — nor dead —
Though hard I strove, but strove in vain
To rend and gnash my bonds in twain.
He died, and they unlocked his chain,
And scooped for him a shallow grave   150
Even from the cold earth of our cave.
I begged them as a boon to lay
His corpse in dust whereon the day
Might shine — it was a foolish thought,
But then within my brain it wrought,   155
That even in death his free-born breast
In such a dungeon could not rest.
I might have spared my idle prayer —
They coldly laughed, and laid him there,
The flat and turfless earth above   160

The being we so much did love;
His empty chain above it leant,
Such murder's fitting monument!

But he, the favorite and the flower,
Most cherished since his natal hour,
His mother's image in fair face,
The infant love of all his race,
His martyred father's dearest thought,
My latest care, for whom I sought

165

To hoard my life, that his might be 170
Less wretched now, and one day free;
He, too, who yet had held untired
A spirit natural or inspired —
He, too, was struck, and day by day
Was withered on the stalk away. 175
Oh, God! it is a fearful thing
To see the human soul take wing
In any shape, in any mood;
I've seen it rushing forth in blood;
I've seen it on the breaking ocean 180
Strive with a swol'n convulsive motion,
I've seen the sick and ghastly bed
Of sin, delirious with its dread;
But these were horrors — this was woe
Unmixed with such — but sure and slow. 185
He faded, and so calm and meek,
So softly worn, so sweetly weak,
So tearless, yet so tender — kind
And grieved for those he left behind;
With all the while a cheek whose bloom 190
Was as a mockery of the tomb,
Whose tints as gently sunk away
As a departing rainbow's ray;
An eye of most transparent light,
That almost made the dungeon bright; 195
And not a word of murmur, not
A groan o'er his untimely lot —
A little talk of better days,
A little hope my own to raise,
For I was sunk in silence — lost 200
In this last loss, of all the most;
And then the sighs he would suppress

Of fainting nature's feebleness,
More slowly drawn, grew less and less;
I listened, but I could not hear;   205
I called, for I was wild with fear;
I knew 'twas hopeless, but my dread
Would not be thus admonishèd;
I called, and thought I heard a sound —
I burst my chain with one strong bound,   210
And rushed to him — I found him not,
I only stirred in this black spot,
I only lived, I only drew
The accursèd breath of dungeon-dew;
The last, the sole, the dearest link   215
Between me and the eternal brink,
Which bound me to my failing race,
Was broken in this fatal place.
One on the earth, and one beneath —
My brothers — both had ceased to breathe.   220
I took that hand which lay so still,
Alas! my own was full as chill;
I had not strength to stir, or strive,
But felt that I was still alive —
A frantic feeling, when we know   225
That what we love shall ne'er be so.
    I know not why
    I could not die,
I had no earthly hope — but faith,
And that forbade a selfish death.   230

What next befell me then and there
    I know not well — I never knew —
First came the loss of light, and air,
    And then of darkness too.

I had no thought, no feeling — none —   235
Among the stones I stood a stone,
And was scarce conscious what I wist,
As shrubless crags within the mist;
For all was blank, and bleak, and gray;
It was not night, it was not day;   240
It was not even the dungeon-light,
So hateful to my heavy sight,
But vacancy absorbing space,
And fixedness without a place;
There were no stars, no earth, no time,   245
No check, no change, no good, no crime,
But silence, and a stirless breath
Which neither was of life nor death;
A sea of stagnant idleness,
Blind, boundless, mute, and motionless!   250

A light broke in upon my brain —
   It was the carol of a bird;
It ceased, and then it came again,
   The sweetest song ear ever heard,
And mine was thankful till my eyes   255
Ran over with the glad surprise,
And they that moment could not see
I was the mate of misery;
But then by dull degrees came back
My senses to their wonted track;   260
I saw the dungeon walls and floor
Close slowly round me as before,
I saw the glimmer of the sun
Creeping as it before had done,
But through the crevice where it came   265
That bird was perched, as fond and tame,

And tamer than upon the tree;
A lovely bird, with azure wings,
And song that said a thousand things,
    And seemed to say them all for me!   270
I never saw its like before,
I ne'er shall see its likeness more;
It seemed like me to want a mate,
But was not half so desolate,
And it was come to love me when   275
None lived to love me so again,
And cheering from my dungeon's brink,
Had brought me back to feel and think.
I know not if it late were free,
    Or broke its cage to perch on mine,   280
But knowing well captivity,
    Sweet bird! I could not wish for thine!
Or if it were, in wingèd guise,
A visitant from Paradise;
For — Heaven forgive that thought! the while   285
Which made me both to weep and smile —
I sometimes deemed that it might be
My brother's soul come down to me;
But then at last away it flew,
And then 'twas mortal well I knew,   290
For he would never thus have flown,
And left me twice so doubly lone,
Lone as the corpse within its shroud,
Lone as a solitary cloud —
    A single cloud on a sunny day,   295
While all the rest of heaven is clear,
    A frown upon the atmosphere,
That hath no business to appear
    When skies are blue, and earth is gay.

A kind of change came in my fate; 300
My keepers grew compassionate;
I know not what had made them so,
They were inured to sights of woe,
But so it was — my broken chain
With links unfastened did remain, 305
And it was liberty to stride
Along my cell from side to side,
And up and down, and then athwart,
And tread it over every part;
And round the pillars one by one, 310
Returning where my walk begun,
Avoiding only, as I trod,
My brothers' graves without a sod;
For if I thought with heedless tread
My step profaned their lowly bed, 315
My breath came gaspingly and thick,
And my crushed heart fell blind and sick.

I made a footing in the wall,
    It was not therefrom to escape,
For I had buried one and all 320
    Who loved me in a human shape;
And the whole earth would henceforth be
A wider prison unto me.
No child, no sire, no kin had I,
No partner in my misery; 325
I thought of this, and I was glad,
For thought of them had made me mad;
But I was curious to ascend
To my barred windows, and to bend
Once more, upon the mountains high, 330
The quiet of a loving eye.

I saw them, and they were the same,
They were not changed like me in frame;
I saw their thousand years of snow
On high — their wide long lake below,   335
And the blue Rhone in fullest flow;
I heard the torrents leap and gush
O'er channeled rock and broken bush;
I saw the white-walled distant town,
And whiter sails go skimming down;   340
And then there was a little isle,
Which in my very face did smile,
    The only one in view;
A small green isle; it seemed no more,
Scarce broader than my dungeon floor,   345
But in it there were three tall trees,
And o'er it blew the mountain breeze,
And by it there were waters flowing,
And on it there were young flowers growing,
    Of gentle breath and hue.   350
The fish swam by the castle wall,
And they seemed joyous each and all;
The eagle rode the rising blast,
Methought he never flew so fast
As then to me he seemed to fly;   355
And then new tears came in my eye,
And I felt troubled — and would fain
I had not left my recent chain;
And when I did descend again,
The darkness of my dim abode   360
Fell on me as a heavy load;
It was as is a new-dug grave,
Closing o'er one we sought to save —

And yet my glance, too much oppressed
Had almost need of such a rest.   365

It might be months, or years, or days;
   I kept no count, I took no note,
I had no hope my eyes to raise,
   And clear them of their dreary mote;
At last men came to set me free;   370
   I asked not why, and recked not where;
It was at length the same to me,
Fettered or fetterless to be,
   I learned to love despair.
And thus when they appeared at last,   375
And all my bonds aside were cast,
These heavy walls to me had grown
A hermitage — and all my own,
And half I felt as they were come
To tear me from a second home;   380
With spiders I had friendship made,
And watched them in their sullen trade,
Had seen the mice by moonlight play,
And why should I feel less than they?
We were all inmates of one place,   385
And I, the monarch of each race,
Had power to kill — yet, strange to tell!
In quiet we had learned to dwell.
My very chains and I grew friends,
So much a long communion tends   390
To make us what we are — even I
Regained my freedom with a sigh.

GEORGE GORDON, LORD BYRON

The Lady of Shalott

*If you know any of the King Arthur legends, the Lady of Shalott
will be familiar to you. In ancient Britain, at Camelot, King Arthur
established his famed court, the Knights of the Round Table. The
noblest of his knights, and his favorite, was Sir Lancelot. Among
Lancelot's admirers was the mysterious Lady of Shalott, but he
moved in a world in which she had no part. The poet Tennyson
makes us feel the sadness of her hopeless love in many ways, chiefly
by the solemn repetition of two lines and the bell-like rhymes —
groups of four and three in every stanza — that seem to toll for the
beautiful lady who came " floating down to Camelot." Here you
will sense the atmosphere of ages gone by, of the days of chivalry,
with mention of such things as greaves (leg shields worn by warriors) and baldric (a shoulder strap from which a curved bugle
hung).*

PART I

On either side the river lie
Long fields of barley and of rye,
That clothe the wold and meet the sky;
And through the field the road runs by
  To many-towered Camelot;   5
And up and down the people go,
Gazing where the lilies blow
Round an island there below,
  The island of Shalott.

Willows whiten, aspens quiver,   10
Little breezes dusk and shiver
Through the wave that runs for ever
By the island in the river
  Flowing down to Camelot.

Four gray walls, and four gray towers,   15
Overlook a space of flowers,
And the silent isle imbowers
      The Lady of Shalott.

By the margin, willow-veiled,
Slide the heavy barges trailed   20
By slow horses; and unhailed
The shallop flitteth silken-sailed
      Skimming down to Camelot;
But who hath seen her wave her hand?
Or at the casement seen her stand?   25
Or is she known in all the land,
      The Lady of Shalott?

Only reapers, reaping early
In among the bearded barley,
Hear a song that echoes cheerly   30
From the river winding clearly,
      Down to towered Camelot:
And by the moon the reaper weary,
Piling sheaves in uplands airy,
Listening, whispers " 'Tis the fairy   35
      Lady of Shalott."

PART II

There she weaves by night and day
A magic web with colors gay.
She has heard a whisper say,
A curse is on her if she stay   40
      To look down to Camelot.
She knows not what the curse may be,
And so she weaveth steadily,

And little other care hath she,
  The Lady of Shalott.   45

And moving through a mirror clear
That hangs before her all the year,
Shadows of the world appear.
There she sees the highway near
   Winding down to Camelot: 50
There the river eddy whirls,
And there the surly village-churls,
And the red cloaks of market-girls,
  Pass onward from Shalott.

Sometimes a troop of damsels glad, 55
An abbot on an ambling pad,
Sometimes a curly shepherd-lad,
Or long-haired page in crimson clad,
   Goes by to towered Camelot;
And sometimes through the mirror blue 60
The knights come riding two and two;
She hath no loyal knight and true,
  The Lady of Shalott.

But in her web she still delights
To weave the mirror's magic sights, 65
For often through the silent nights
A funeral, with plumes and lights
   And music, went to Camelot:
Or when the moon was overhead,
Came two young lovers lately wed; 70
"I am half-sick of shadows," said
  The Lady of Shalott.

PART III

A bow-shot from her bower-eaves,
He rode between the barley sheaves,
The sun came dazzling through the leaves,   75
And flamed upon the brazen greaves
      Of bold Sir Lancelot.
A red-cross knight for ever kneeled
To a lady in his shield,
That sparkled on the yellow field,   80
      Beside remote Shalott.

The gemmy bridle glittered free,
Like to some branch of stars we see
Hung in the golden Galaxy.
The bridle-bells rang merrily   85
      As he rode down to Camelot:
And from his blazoned baldric slung
A mighty silver bugle hung,
And as he rode his armor rung,
      Beside remote Shalott.   90

All in the blue unclouded weather
Thick-jeweled shone the saddle-leather,
The helmet and the helmet-feather
Burned like one burning flame together,
      As he rode down to Camelot.   95
As often through the purple night,
Below the starry clusters bright,
Some bearded meteor, trailing light,
      Moves over still Shalott.

His broad clear brow in sunlight glowed;   100
On burnished hooves his war-horse trode;

From underneath his helmet flowed
His coal-black curls as on he rode,
      As he rode down to Camelot.
From the bank and from the river   105
He flashed into the crystal mirror,
" Tirra lirra," by the river
      Sang Sir Lancelot.

She left the web, she left the loom,
She made three paces through the room.   110
She saw the water-lily bloom,
She saw the helmet and the plume,
      She looked down to Camelot.
Out flew the web and floated wide!
The mirror cracked from side to side!   115
" The curse is come upon me," cried
      The Lady of Shalott.

PART IV

In the stormy east-wind straining,
The pale-yellow woods were waning,
The broad stream in his banks complaining,   120
Heavily the low sky raining
      Over towered Camelot!
Down she came and found a boat
Beneath a willow left afloat,
And round about the prow she wrote   125
      The Lady of Shalott.

And down the river's dim expanse —
Like some bold seër in a trance,
Seeing all his own mischance —
With a glassy countenance   130
      Did she look to Camelot.

And at the closing of the day
She loosed the chain, and down she lay!
The broad stream bore her far away,
   The Lady of Shalott.   135

Lying, robed in snowy white
That loosely flew to left and right —
The leaves upon her falling light —
Through the noises of the night
   She floated down to Camelot: 140
And as the boat-head wound along
The willowy hills and fields among,
They heard her singing her last song,
   The Lady of Shalott.

Heard a carol, mournful, holy,   145
Chanted loudly, chanted lowly,
Till her blood was frozen slowly,
And her eyes were darkened wholly,
   Turned to towered Camelot!
For ere she reached upon the tide. 150
The first house by the water-side,
Singing in her song she died,
   The Lady of Shalott.

Under tower and balcony,
By garden-wall and gallery,   155
A gleaming shape she floated by,
A corpse between the houses high,
   Silent into Camelot.
Out upon the wharfs they came,
Knight and burgher, lord and dame, 160
And round the prow they read her name,
   The Lady of Shalott.

Who is this? and what is here?
And in the lighted palace near
Died the sound of royal cheer;   165
And they crossed themselves for fear,
    All the knights at Camelot:
But Lancelot mused a little space:
He said, " She has a lovely face!
God in his mercy lend her grace,   170
    The Lady of Shalott."

ALFRED TENNYSON

The Song of the Shirt

Thomas Hood was an English humorist whose light verse can be found in countless collections. Yet when Hood wrote on a serious subject his lines carried a message of deep significance. Such a poem is " The Song of the Shirt," which tells of the cruel use of overworked laborers — most of them women and children — during the early nineteenth century. Hood wrote the poem after reading a newspaper account of a seamstress on trial for pawning articles that belonged to her employer. It was revealed that she earned only seven shillings for a full week's labor — less than two dollars in our money today.

With fingers weary and worn,
   With eyelids heavy and red,
A woman sat, in unwomanly rags,
   Plying her needle and thread —
     Stitch — stitch — stitch!
In poverty, hunger, and dirt,   5
    And still with a voice of dolorous pitch
She sang the " Song of the Shirt! "

" Work — work — work!
While the cock is crowing aloof;   10
   And work — work — work
Till the stars shine through the roof!
It's oh! to be a slave
   Along with the barbarous Turk,
Where woman has never a soul to save   15
   If this is Christian work!

" Work — work — work
Till the brain begins to swim;
   Work — work — work
Till the eyes are heavy and dim!   20
Seam, and gusset, and band, —
   Band, and gusset, and seam,
Till over the buttons I fall asleep,
   And sew them on in a dream!

" O! men with sisters dear!   25
   O! men with mothers and wives!
It is not linen you're wearing out,
   But human creatures' lives!
     Stitch — stitch — stitch,
   In poverty, hunger, and dirt,   30
Sewing at once, with a double thread,
   A shroud as well as a shirt.

" But why do I talk of death!
   That phantom of grisly bone,
I hardly fear his terrible shape,   35
   It seems so like my own —

It seems so like my own,
  Because of the fasts I keep;
O God! that bread should be so dear,
  And flesh and blood so cheap!   40

" Work — work — work!
  My labor never flags;
And what are its wages? A bed of straw,
  A crust of bread — and rags.
That shattered roof, — and this naked floor, —   45
  A table, — a broken chair, —
And a wall so blank, my shadow I thank
  For sometimes falling there.

  " Work — work — work!
From weary chime to chime,   50
  Work — work — work —
As prisoners work for crime!
  Band, and gusset, and seam,
  Seam, and gusset, and band,
Till the heart is sick, and the brain benumbed,   55
  As well as the weary hand.

  " Work — work — work,
In the dull December light,
  And work — work — work,
When the weather is warm and bright —   60
While underneath the eaves
  The brooding swallows cling,
As if to show me their sunny backs
  And twit me with the Spring.

  " Oh! but to breathe the breath   65
Of the cowslip and primrose sweet —

With the sky above my head,
And the grass beneath my feet,
For only one short hour
    To feel as I used to feel,   70
Before I knew the woes of want
    And the walk that costs a meal!

" Oh! but for one short hour!
    A respite however brief!
No blessed leisure for love or hope,   75
    But only time for grief!
A little weeping would ease my heart,
    But in their briny bed
My tears must stop, for every drop
    Hinders needle and thread! "   80

With fingers weary and worn,
    With eyelids heavy and red,
A woman sat, in unwomanly rags,
    Plying her needle and thread —
        Stitch — stitch — stitch!   85
    In poverty, hunger, and dirt,
And still with a voice of dolorous pitch, —
Would that its tone could reach the rich!
She sang this " Song of the Shirt! "

THOMAS HOOD

Lucy

Poetry is the most condensed form of writing; it can pack a whole biography in a few lines. Wordsworth reveals the shy nature of a simple country girl in the three stanzas of " Lucy." Emily Dickinson tells us a great deal about herself in the eight lines of " A Nobody," which follows this poem.

She dwelt among the untrodden ways
   Beside the springs of Dove,
A maid whom there were none to praise
   And very few to love:

A violet by a mossy stone
   Half hidden from the eye!
Fair as a star, when only one
   Is shining in the sky.

She lived unknown, and few could know
   When Lucy ceased to be;
But she is in her grave, and oh,
   The difference to me!

WILLIAM WORDSWORTH

A Nobody

I'm nobody! Who are you?
Are you nobody, too?
Then there's a pair of us — don't tell!
They'd banish us, you know.

How dreary to be somebody!
How public, like a frog
To tell your name the livelong day
To an admiring bog!

EMILY DICKINSON

4
OUR AMERICAN
HERITAGE

George Washington

If he had not become the father of his country, George Washington might have been an English sailor, a wealthy country gentleman, or King of America. But fate had other plans for him. Still — as this poem points out with a touch of humor — it is well to remember the important decisions that made the Virginia surveyor and landowner " first in war, first in peace, first in the hearts of his countrymen."

Sing hey! for bold George Washington
That jolly British tar;
King George's famous admiral
From Hull to Zanzibar!
No — wait a minute — something's wrong —   5
George *wished* to sail the foam.
But, when his mother thought, aghast,
Of Georgie shinning up a mast,
Her tears and protests flowed so fast
That George remained at home.   10

Sing ho! for grave George Washington,
The staid Virginia squire,

Who farms his fields and hunts his hounds
And aims at nothing higher!
Stop, stop, it's going wrong again!   15
George *liked* to live on farms,
But, when the Colonies agreed
They could and should and would be freed,
They called on George to do the deed,
And George cried " Shoulder arms! "   20

Sing ha! for Emperor Washington,
That hero of renown,
Who freed his land from Britain's rule
To win a golden crown!
No, no, that's what George *might* have won   25
But didn't, for he said,
" There's not much point about a king,
They're pretty but they're apt to sting;
And, as for crowns — the heavy thing
Would only hurt my head."   30

Sing ho! for our George Washington!
(At last I've got it straight.)
The first in war, the first in peace,
The goodly and the great.
But, when you think about him now,   35
From here to Valley Forge,
Remember this — he might have been
A highly different specimen,
And, where on earth would we be, then?
I'm glad that George was George.

ROSEMARY AND STEPHEN VINCENT BENÉT

Daniel Boone

It is difficult to separate the real Daniel Boone from the legendary figure he has become. He was born in 1735 in Bucks County, Pennsylvania, moved to North Carolina, and was one of the first to explore the great wilderness of Kentucky. But the plain facts of Boone's life are dwarfed by the fictional stories in which he is glorified. Legends clustered about his name even before he died and, as with Davy Crockett, many tall tales, told and retold through the years, have made him a folk hero.

This poem is a mixture of fact and fancy about Daniel Boone. There is the real Boone, a woodsman making a road through the woods, winning his way against the Indians who were allied with the British against the colonists. There is also the Boone of myth and tale, a giant striding the frontier, searching restlessly for a wider world, a world without bounds. The poet fancies him riding mythical creatures after he is done with pioneering in this life, hunting fabulous monsters across the skies — always with his American cry of " Elbow room! "

Daniel Boone at twenty-one
Came with his tomahawk, knife, and gun
Home from the French and Indian War
To North Carolina and the Yadkin shore.
He married his maid with a golden band,   5
Builded his house and cleared his land;
But the deep woods claimed their son again
And he turned his face from the homes of men.
Over the Blue Ridge, dark and lone,
The Mountains of Iron, the Hills of Stone,   10
Braving the Shawnee's jealous wrath,
He made his way on the Warrior's Path.
Alone he trod the shadowed trails;

But he was lord of a thousand vales
As he roved Kentucky, far and near,   15
Hunting the buffalo, elk, and deer.
What joy to see, what joy to win
So fair a land for his kith and kin,
Of streams unstained and woods unhewn!
"Elbow room!" laughed Daniel Boone.   20

On the Wilderness Road that his axmen made
The settlers flocked to the first stockade;
The deerskin shirts and the coonskin caps
Filed through the glens and the mountain gaps;
And hearts were high in the fateful spring   25
When the land said "Nay!" to the stubborn king.
While the men of the East of farms and town
Strove with the troops of the British Crown,
Daniel Boone from a surge of hate
Guarded a nation's westward gate.   30
Down in the fort in a wave of flame
The Shawnee horde and the Mingo came,
And the stout logs shook in a storm of lead;
But Boone stood firm and the savage fled.
Peace! and the settlers flocked anew,   35
The farm lands spread, the town lands grew;
But Daniel Boone was ill at ease
When he saw smoke in his forest trees.
"There'll be no game in the country soon.
Elbow room!" cried Daniel Boone.   40

Straight as a pine at sixty-five —
Time enough for a man to thrive —
He launched his bateau on Ohio's breast
And his heart was glad as he oared it west;

There was kindly folk and his own true blood   45
Where great Missouri rolls his flood;
New woods, new streams, and room to spare,
And Daniel Boone found comfort there.

Yet far he ranged toward the sunset still,
Where the Kansas runs and the Smoky Hill,   50
And the prairies toss, by the south wind blown;
And he killed his bear on the Yellowstone.
But ever he dreamed of new domains
With vaster woods and wider plains;
Ever he dreamed of a world-to-be   55
Where there are no bounds and the soul is free.

At fourscore-five, still stout and hale,
He heard a call to a farther trail;
So he turned his face where the stars are strewn;
" Elbow room! " sighed Daniel Boone.   60

Down the Milky Way in its banks of blue
Far he has paddled his white canoe
To the splendid quest of the tameless soul —
He has reached the goal where there is no goal.
Now he rides and rides an endless trail   65
On the hippogriff of the flaming tail
Or the horse of the stars with the golden mane,
As he rode the first of the blue-grass strain.
The joy that lies in the search he seeks
On breathless hills with crystal peaks;   70
He makes his camp on heights untrod,
The steps of the shrine, alone with God.
Through the woods of the vast, on the plains of space
He hunts the pride of the mammoth race
And the dinosaur of the triple horn,   75
The manticore and the unicorn,
As once by the broad Missouri's flow
He followed the elk and the buffalo.
East of the sun and west of the moon,
" Elbow room! " laughs Daniel Boone.

ARTHUR GUITERMAN

Andrew Jackson

*Hard of muscle and tough in spirit, Andrew Jackson was given a
nickname that fitted the man. " Old Hickory " they called him.
Raised in the wild country, " a regular Western fighting-cock," his*

*eyes were sharp as a forest animal's and his mind was quick as a
trigger. He fought a number of duels, commanded a series of campaigns against the Creek Indians, and captured the Spanish town
of Pensacola. In 1815, at the end of the War of 1812, his victory at
New Orleans, where the British lost their commander and 2000
soldiers, was accomplished at a cost of only eight men. Even Jackson's married life was a source of fight and bloodshed. His enemies
said that his wife, a Mrs. Rachel Robards, had not been legally di-
vorced from her first husband at the time Jackson married her and,
though the marriage ceremony was performed a second time, Jackson was extremely sensitive about the gossip. As President for two
terms, he was cheered and loyally supported by the common people as one of themselves — Old Hickory!*

> He was a man as hot as whiskey.
> He was a man whose word was good.
> He was a man whose hate was risky —
>   Andrew Jackson — hickory wood!

> He was in love with love and glory;   5
> His hopes were prospered, but at a price:
> The bandying of the ugly story
>   He'd had to marry his Rachel twice.

> Hot he was and a hasty suitor,
> But if he sinned he was poor at sin.   10
> She was plain as a spoon of pewter,
>   Plain and good as a safety pin.

> Andrew Jackson, man of honor,
> Held her name like he held his head.
> He stopped a bullet for slurs upon her.   15
>   All his life he carried lead.

All his life wherever he went he
Wore the scar of a pistol shot —
Along with others he had in plenty.
    Hickory wood is hard to rot.   20

Hard to rot and a fiery fuel —
When faith and freedom both burned dim,
He stood his guns as he fought a duel,
    And heartened others to stand with him.

With any man who was good at sighting,   25
No ally but the thief Lafitte,
And no campaigns but Indian fighting —
    He brought the British to black defeat.

The odds against him were more than double.
His gunmounts sank like a heart that fails,   30
Sank in mud and the frosty stubble —
    So he set his cannon on cotton bales.

And over the cane and the silver sedges —
The redcoats' coats were as red as flame —
In a hundred rows like a hundred hedges,   35
    The bayonets of the British came.

The smoke of his cannon rolled and scattered
Like bursting flowers, like cotton blooms.
Like teeth from a comb the red ranks shattered,
    While water lifted in yellow plumes.   40

White and red on the silver carpet,
Scarlet tunics by crossbelts crossed,
They fell and died — and a flood of scarlet
    Covered over the field of frost.

He was a man whose hand was steady.   45
He was a man whose aim was good.
He was a man whose guns were ready —
   Andrew Jackson — hickory wood!

MARTHA KELLER

An Old-Time Sea-Fight

In the midst of a long poem entitled " Song of Myself," Walt Whitman described the climax of a great naval battle. He did not go into detail about the battle, nor even name the hero. The action is flashed before the reader in brief but brilliant illuminations.

At the beginning of the Revolutionary War, the foremost among Colonial naval captains was John Paul Jones, a Scottish sailor who had joined the American forces. His ship flew the first flag of the Revolution: a pine tree with a snake at its base, bearing the motto, " Don't tread on me!" On Sept. 23, 1779, his small squadron encountered a British fleet and gave chase. His flagship, the Bon Homme Richard, *was attacked by the British* Serapis, *a greatly superior ship carrying forty-four guns. At first the* Serapis *seemed invincible, but even though his boat was sinking, Jones succeeded in lashing it fast to the enemy vessel and, when called upon to surrender, replied, " I have not yet begun to fight!" At the end of two hours, the* Serapis *was on fire from stem to stern; half an hour later she surrendered.*

Would you hear of an old-time sea-fight?
Would you learn who won by the light of the moon and stars?
List to the yarn, as my grandmother's father the sailor told it
   to me.

Our foe was no skulk in his ship I tell you, (said he,)
His was the surly English pluck, and there is no tougher or
   truer, and never was, and never will be;   5
Along the lowered eve he came horribly raking us.

We closed with him, the yards entangled, the cannon touched,
My captain lashed fast with his own hands.

We had received some eighteen pound shots under the water,
On our lower-gun-deck two large pieces had burst at the first
    fire, killing all around and blowing up overhead.   10

Fighting at sun-down, fighting at dark,
Ten o'clock at night, the full moon well up, our leaks on the
    gain, and five feet of water reported,
The master-at-arms loosing the prisoners confined in the after-
    hold to give them a chance for themselves.
The transit to and from the magazine is now stopped by the
    sentinels,
They see so many strange faces they do not know whom to
    trust.   15

Our frigate takes fire,
The other asks if we demand quarter?
If our colors are struck and the fighting done?

Now I laugh content, for I hear the voice of my little captain,
We have not struck, he composedly cries, *we have just begun
    our part of the fighting.*   20

Only three guns are in use,
One is directed by the captain himself against the enemy's
    mainmast,
Two well served with grape and canister silence his musketry
    and clear his decks.

The tops alone second the fire of this little battery, especially
    the main-top,
They hold out bravely during the whole of the action.   25

Not a moment's cease.
The leaks gain fast on the pumps, the fire eats toward the
    powder-magazine.

One of the pumps has been shot away, it is generally thought
    we are sinking.

Serene stands the little captain,
He is not hurried, his voice is neither high nor low,   30
His eyes give more light to us than our battle-lanterns.

Toward twelve there in the beams of the moon they surrender
    to us.

WALT WHITMAN

Old Ironsides

During the War of 1812 the American warship Constitution *often
fought against great odds and in one battle, when enemy shells
were seen ricocheting off her, she earned the name " Old Ironsides." In 1830 inspectors concluded that the ship's career was
over and the Secretary of the Navy ordered the vessel destroyed.
This came to the attention of the New England poet, Oliver
Wendell Holmes, who sat down and wrote a sad and angry poem
which was so often repeated that it became a cry of protest. Finally,
there was so much public feeling that, instead of being broken up
by " the harpies of the shore," men who would profit from the
transaction, " Old Ironsides " was rebuilt.*

Ay, tear her tattered ensign down!
    Long has it waved on high,
And many an eye has danced to see
    That banner in the sky;
Beneath it rung the battle-shout,   5

And burst the cannon's roar:
The meteor of the ocean air
Shall sweep the clouds no more!

Her deck, once red with heroes' blood,
Where knelt the vanquished foe,   10
When winds were hurrying o'er the flood
And waves were white below,

No more shall feel the victor's tread,
Or know the conquered knee:
The harpies of the shore shall pluck   15
The eagle of the sea!

O better that her shattered hulk
Should sink beneath the wave!
Her thunders shook the mighty deep,
And there should be her grave: 20
Nail to the mast her holy flag,
Set every threadbare sail,
And give her to the god of storms,
The lightning and the gale!

OLIVER WENDELL HOLMES

Barbara Frietchie

" Barbara Frietchie " is a story-poem which has become part of the lore of our nation. Some historians claim that the event is fictitious; others insist that it actually occurred during the War between the States, when General Lee's army marched through Frederick, Maryland.

Up from the meadows rich with corn,
Clear in the cool September morn,

The clustered spires of Frederick stand
Green-walled by the hills of Maryland.

Round about them orchards sweep,   5
Apple and peach tree fruited deep,

Fair as a garden of the Lord
To the eyes of the famished rebel horde,

On that pleasant morn of the early fall
When Lee marched over the mountain wall, —   10

Over the mountains, winding down,
Horse and foot into Frederick town.

Forty flags with their silver stars,
Forty flags with their crimson bars,

Flapped in the morning wind; the sun   15
Of noon looked down, and saw not one.

Up rose old Barbara Frietchie then,
Bowed with her fourscore years and ten;

Bravest of all in Frederick town,
She took up the flag the men hauled down;   20

In her attic-window the staff she set,
To show that one heart was loyal yet.

Up the street came the rebel tread,
Stonewall Jackson riding ahead.

Under his slouched hat left and right   25
He glanced: the old flag met his sight.

" Halt! " — the dust-brown ranks stood fast;
" Fire " — out blazed the rifle-blast.

It shivered the window, pane and sash;
It rent the banner with seam and gash.   30

Quick, as it fell, from the broken staff
Dame Barbara snatched the silken scarf;

She leaned far out on the window-sill,
And shook it forth with a royal will.

" Shoot, if you must, this old gray head,   35
But spare your country's flag," she said.

A shade of sadness, a blush of shame,
Over the face of the leader came;

The nobler nature within him stirred
To life at that woman's deed and word: 40

" Who touches a hair of yon gray head
Dies like a dog! March on! " he said.

All day long through Frederick street
Sounded the tread of marching feet;

All day long that free flag tossed   45
Over the heads of the rebel host.

Ever its torn folds rose and fell
On the loyal winds that loved it well;

And through the hill-gaps sunset light
Shone over it with a warm good-night.   50

Barbara Frietchie's work is o'er,
And the rebel rides on his raids no more.

Honor to her! and let a tear
Fall, for her sake, on Stonewall's bier.

Over Barbara Frietchie's grave,   55
Flag of Freedom and Union, wave!

Peace and order and beauty draw
Round thy symbol of light and law;

And ever the stars above look down
On thy stars below in Frederick town!

JOHN GREENLEAF WHITTIER

Little Giffen

The pages of history books are crowded with the names of generals,
admirals, and statesmen, yet history is often made by little-known
people. Occasionally one of these ordinary people emerges from
the ranks to win our admiration. Such a hero was the young boy
depicted in Robert Browning's poem "Incident in a French
Camp," on p. 90. His American counterpart, Little Giffen of Ten-
nessee, was a Confederate soldier who lay wounded and covered
with sores like Lazarus in the Bible story, but rose to duty and re-
turned to battle.

Out of the focal and foremost fire,
Out of the hospital walls as dire;
Smitten of grapeshot and gangrene,
(Eighteenth battle, and *he* sixteen!)
Little Giffen, of Tennessee!   5

" Take him and welcome! " the surgeons said;
Little the doctor can help the dead!
So we took him; and brought him where
The balm was sweet in the summer air;
And we laid him down on a wholesome bed —   10
Utter Lazarus, heel to head!

And we watched the war with bated breath —
Skeleton boy against skeleton death.
Months of torture, how many such?
Weary weeks of the stick and crutch;   15
And still a glint of the steel-blue eye
Told of the spirit that wouldn't die,
And didn't. Nay, more! in death's despite
The crippled skeleton " learned to write."
" Dear mother," at first, of course; and then   20
" Dear captain," inquiring about the men.
Captain's answer: " Of eighty and five,
Giffen and I are left alive."

Word of gloom from the war, one day;
Johnston pressed at the front, they say.   25
Little Giffen was up and away;
A tear — his first — as he bade good-by,
Dimmed the glint of his steel-blue eye.
" I'll write, if spared! " There was news of the fight;
But none of Giffen. He did not write.   30

I sometimes fancy that, were I king
Of the princely knights of the Golden Ring,
With the songs of the minstrel in mine ear,
And the tender legend that trembles here,

> I'd give the best on his bended knee,   35
> The whitest soul of my chivalry,
> For " Little Giffen " of Tennessee.

FRANCIS ORRAY TICKNOR

Kentucky Belle

Summer of 'sixty-three, sir, and Conrad was gone away —
Gone to the county town, sir, to sell our first load of hay.
We live in the log house yonder, poor as ever you've seen;
Röschen there was a baby, and I was only nineteen.

Conrad, he took the oxen, but he left Kentucky Belle;   5
How much we thought of Kentuck, I couldn't begin to tell —
Came from the Bluegrass country; my father gave her to me
When I rode north with Conrad, away from the Tennessee.

Conrad lived in Ohio — a German he is, you know —
The house stood in broad cornfields, stretching on, row after
  row;   10
The old folks made me welcome; they were kind as kind could
  be;
But I kept longing, longing, for the hills of the Tennessee.

O, for a sight of water, the shadowed slope of a hill!
Clouds that hang on the summit, a wind that never is still!
But the level land went stretching away to meet the sky —   15
Never a rise, from north to south, to rest the weary eye!

From east to west, no river to shine out under the moon,
Nothing to make a shadow in the yellow afternoon;

Only the breathless sunshine, as I looked out, all forlorn,
Only the " rustle, rustle," as I walked among the corn.   20

When I fell sick with pining we didn't wait any more,
But moved away from the cornlands out to this river shore —
The Tuscarawas it's called, sir — off there's a hill, you see —
And now I've grown to like it next best to the Tennessee.   24

I was at work that morning. Someone came riding like mad
Over the bridge and up the road — Farmer Rouf's little lad.
Bareback he rode; he had no hat; he hardly stopped to say,
" Morgan's men are coming, Frau, they're galloping on this
     way.

" I'm sent to warn the neighbors. He isn't a mile behind;   29
He sweeps up all the horses — every horse that he can find;
Morgan, Morgan the raider, and Morgan's terrible men,
With bowie knives and pistols, are galloping up the glen."

The lad rode down the valley, and I stood still at the door —
The baby laughed and prattled, playing with spools on the
     floor;
Kentuck was out in the pasture; Conrad, my man, was gone;
Near, near Morgan's men were galloping, galloping on!   36

Sudden I picked up baby and ran to the pasture bar:
" Kentuck! " I called; " Kentucky! " She knew me ever so far!
I led her down the gully that turns off there to the right,
And tied her to the bushes; her head was just out of sight.   40

As I ran back to the log house at once there came a sound —
The ring of hoofs, galloping hoofs, trembling over the ground,

Coming into the turnpike out from the White-Woman
    Glen —
Morgan, Morgan the raider, and Morgan's terrible men.

As near they drew and nearer my heart beat fast in alarm;   45
But still I stood in the doorway, with baby on my arm.
They came; they passed; with spur and whip in haste they sped
    along;
Morgan, Morgan the raider, and his band six hundred strong.

Weary they looked and jaded, riding through night and
    through day;
Pushing on east to the river, many long miles away,   50
To the border strip where Virginia runs up into the west,
And for the Upper Ohio before they could stop to rest.

On like the wind they hurried, and Morgan rode in advance;
Bright were his eyes like live coals, as he gave me a sideways
    glance;
And I was just breathing freely, after my choking pain,   55
When the last one of the troopers suddenly drew his rein.

Frightened I was to death, sir; I scarce dared look in his face,
As he asked for a drink of water and glanced around the place;
I gave him a cup, and he smiled — 'twas only a boy, you see,
Faint and worn, with his blue eyes; and he'd sailed on the
    Tennessee.   60

Only sixteen he was, sir — a fond mother's only son —
Off and away with Morgan before his life had begun!
The damp drops stood on his temples; drawn was the boyish
    mouth;
And I thought me of the mother waiting down in the South!

O, plucky was he to the backbone and clear grit through and
    through;   65
Boasted and bragged like a trooper; but the big words wouldn't
    do;
The boy was dying, sir, dying, as plain as plain could be,
Worn out by his ride with Morgan up from the Tennessee.

But, when I told the laddie that I too was from the South,
Water came in his dim eyes and quivers around his mouth.
" Do you know the Bluegrass country? " he wistful began to
    say,   71
Then swayed like a willow sapling and fainted dead away.

I had him into the log house, and worked and brought him to;
I fed him and coaxed him, as I thought his mother'd do;
And, when the lad got better, and the noise in his head was
    gone,   75
Morgan's men were miles away, galloping, galloping on.

" O, I must go," he muttered; " I must be up and away!
Morgan, Morgan is waiting for me! O, what will Morgan
    say? "
But I heard a sound of tramping and kept him back from the
    door —
The ringing sound of horses' hoofs that I had heard before.

And on, on came the soldiers — the Michigan cavalry —   81
And fast they rode, and black they looked galloping rapidly;
They had followed hard on Morgan's track; they had followed
    day and night;
But of Morgan and Morgan's raiders they had never caught a
    sight.

And rich Ohio sat startled through all those summer days,   85
For strange, wild men were galloping over her broad highways;
Now here, now there, now seen, now gone, now north, now
    east, now west,
Through river valleys and corn-land farms, sweeping away her
    best.

A bold ride and a long ride! But they were taken at last.
They almost reached the river by galloping hard and fast;   90
But the boys in blue were upon them ere ever they gained the
    ford,
And Morgan, Morgan the raider, laid down his terrible sword.

Well, I kept the boy till evening — kept him against his will —
But he was too weak to follow, and sat there pale and still;
When it was cool and dusky — you'll wonder to hear me
    tell —   95
But I stole down to that gully and brought up Kentucky Belle.

I kissed the star on her forehead — my pretty, gentle lass —
But I knew that she'd be happy back in the old Bluegrass;
A suit of clothes of Conrad's, with all the money I had,
And Kentuck, pretty Kentuck, I gave to the worn-out lad.

I guided him to the southward as well as I knew how;   101
The boy rode off with many thanks, and many a backward
    bow;
And then the glow it faded, and my heart began to swell,
As down the glen away she went, my lost Kentucky Belle!

When Conrad came in the evening the moon was shining
    high;   105
Baby and I were both crying — I couldn't tell him why —

But a battered suit of rebel gray was hanging on the wall,
And a thin old horse with drooping head stood in Kentucky's
    stall.

Well, he was kind, and never once said a hard word to me;
He knew I couldn't help it — 'twas all for the Tennessee;   110
But, after the war was over, just think what came to pass —
A letter, sir; and the two were safe back in the old Bluegrass.

The lad had got across the border, riding Kentucky Belle;
And Kentuck she was thriving, and fat, and hearty, and well;
He cared for her, and kept her, nor touched her with whip
    or spur: 115
Ah! we've had many horses, but never a horse like her!

CONSTANCE FENIMORE WOOLSON

Jim Bludso

Said to be founded on fact, this plain-spoken poem is a dramatic picture of the old days when river boats plied up and down the Mississippi. Their beauty as well as their speed led to great rivalry among the pilots, crews, and engineers, and desperate races were a common occurrence. "Jim Bludso" is the tale of one such race. And behind the tale is an unforgettable man, an ordinary engineer who, like "Casey Jones," became a folk hero.

Wall, no! I can't tell whar he lives,
    Bekase he don't live, you see;
Leastways, he's got out of the habit
    Of livin' like you an' me.
Whar have you been for the last three year   5
    That you haven't heard folks tell
How Jimmy Bludso passed in his checks
    The night of the *Prairie Belle?*

He weren't no saint — them engineers
   Is pretty much all alike —   10
One wife in Natchez-under-the-Hill
   And another one here in Pike;
A keerless man in his talk was Jim,
   And an awkward hand in a row,
But he never flunked, an' he never lied —   15
   I reckon he never knowed how.

And this was all the religion he had —
   To treat his engine well;
Never be passed on the river;
   To mind the pilot's bell;   20

And if ever the *Prairie Belle* took fire,
   A thousand times he swore
He'd hold her nozzle agin the bank
   Till the last soul got ashore.

All the boats has their day on the Mississip',   25
   And her day come at last, —
The *Movastar* was a better boat,
   But the *Belle* she wouldn't be passed.
And so she come tearin' along that night —
   The oldest craft on the line —   30
With a fellow squat on her safety-valve,
   And her furnace crammed, rosin an' pine.

The fire bust out as she cl'ared the bar
   And burned a hole in the night,
And quick as a flash she turned, an' made   35
   For that willer-bank on the right.
There was runnin' an cursin', but Jim yelled out
   Over all the infernal roar,
" I'll hold her nozzle agin the bank
    Till the last galoot's ashore! "
   40

Through the hot black breath of the burnin' boat
   Jim Bludso's voice was heard,
An' they all had trust in his cussedness,
   And knowed he would keep his word.
And, sure's you're born, they all got off   45
   Afore the smokestack fell, —
And Bludso's ghost went up alone
   In the smoke of the *Prairie Belle.*

He weren't no saint — but at Jedgment
  I'd run my chance with Jim,   50
'Longside of some pious gentlemen
  That wouldn't shook hands with him.
He seen his duty, a dead-sure thing, —
  And went for it, thar an' then:
And Christ ain't a-goin' to be too hard   55
  On a man that died for men.

JOHN HAY

5

SIX
FABLES

The Boy and the Wolf

Fables are among the oldest forms of storytelling. Many of those which originated in ancient Greece and the Orient are about animals with human characteristics — and all of them end with a " moral." But the little sermons are delivered so lightly and the lessons are taught with such humor that fables like this and the ones that follow it have delighted people for more than twenty centuries.

A boy employed to guard the sheep
Despised his work. He liked to sleep.
And when a lamb was lost, he'd shout,
" Wolf! Wolf! The wolves are all about! "

The neighbors searched from noon till nine,   5
But of the beast there was no sign.
Yet " Wolf! " he cried next morning when
The villagers came out again.

One evening around six o'clock
A real wolf fell upon the flock.   10
" Wolf! " yelled the boy. " A wolf indeed! "
But no one paid him any heed.

Although he screamed to wake the dead,
" He's fooled us every time," they said,

And let the hungry wolf enjoy   15
His feast of mutton, lamb — and boy.

THE MORAL's this: The man who's wise
Does not defend himself with lies.
Liars are not believed, forsooth,
Even when liars tell the truth.

FROM THE GREEK OF ÆSOP
Adapted by Louis Untermeyer

The Greedy Fox and the Elusive Grapes

A strolling fox, famished and underfed,
    Although he longed for meat, could not resist
A bunch of grapes which hung above his head.
    Licking his lips, he crouched, and jumped — and missed.

"They're higher than I thought," he seemed to muse.   5
    "But those grapes will be all the sweeter when
I cram them down and crush their purple juice."
    And so he sprang up high — and missed again.

Once more he leaped, and one more time he missed.
    Then in disgust he left that leafy bower.   10
"Fruits are enough to make you sick," he hissed.
    "Besides, I'm pretty sure those grapes are sour."

THE MORAL's this: "A fox is no one's fool,"
    He said, "but greed deceived me. Let me teach
A little lesson learned in Nature's school:
    Don't try for things *too* far beyond your reach!"   15

FROM THE GREEK OF ÆSOP
Adapted by Louis Untermeyer

The Frogs Who Wanted a King

The frogs were living happy as could be
  In a wet marsh to which they all were suited;
From every form of trouble they were free,
  And all night long they croaked, and honked, and hooted.
But one fine day a bull-frog said, " The thing   5
" We've never had and *must* have is a king."

So all the frogs immediately prayed;
  " Great Jove," they chorused from their swampy border,
" Send us a king and he will be obeyed,
  A king to bring a rule of Law and Order."   10
Jove heard and chuckled. That night in the bog
There fell a large and most impressive Log.

The swamp was silent; nothing breathed. At first
  The badly frightened frogs did never *once* stir;
But gradually some neared and even durst   15
  To touch and even dance upon the monster.
Whereat they croaked again, " Great Jove, oh hear!
Send us a *living* king, a king to fear."

Once more Jove smiled, and sent them down a Stork.
  " Long live — ! " they croaked. But ere they framed the sen-
    tence,   20
The Stork bent down and, scorning knife or fork,
  Swallowed them all, with no time for repentance!

    THE MORAL's this: No matter what your lot,
      It might be worse. Be glad with what you've got.

FROM THE GREEK OF ÆSOP
Adapted by Joseph Lauren

The Crow and the Fox

A Crow sat perched upon an oak,
   And in his beak he held a cheese.
   A Fox snuffed up the savory breeze,
And thus in honeyed accent spoke:

" O Prince of Crows, such grace of mien   5
Has never in these parts been seen.
If but your song be half as good,
You're the best singer in the wood! "

The Crow, beside himself with pleasure,
   And eager to display his voice,   10
Opened his beak, and dropped his treasure.
   The Fox was on it in a trice.

" Learn, sir," said he, " that flatterers live
On those who swallow what they say.
A cheese is not too much to give   15
For such a piece of sound advice."
The Crow, ashamed to have been such easy prey,
Swore, but too late, no one would catch him twice!

FROM THE FRENCH OF JEAN DE LA FONTAINE
Translated by Edward Marsh

The Blind Men and the Elephant

It was six men of Indostan
   To learning much inclined,
Who went to see the Elephant
   (Though all of them were blind),
That each by observation   5
   Might satisfy his mind.

The *First* approached the Elephant,
   And happening to fall
Against his broad and sturdy side,
   At once began to bawl: 10
" God bless me! but the Elephant
   Is very like a wall! "

The *Second*, feeling of the tusk,
   Cried, " Ho! what have we here
So very round and smooth and sharp?   15
   To me 'tis mighty clear
This wonder of an Elephant
   Is very like a spear! "

The *Third* approached the animal,
   And happening to take   20
The squirming trunk within his hands,
   Thus boldly up and spake:
" I see," quoth he, " the Elephant
   Is very like a snake! "

The *Fourth* reached out an eager hand,   25
   And felt about the knee.
" What most this wondrous beast is like
   Is mighty plain," quoth he;
" 'Tis clear enough the Elephant
   Is very like a tree! "   30

The *Fifth* who chanced to touch the ear,
   Said: " E'en the blindest man
Can tell what this resembles most;
   Deny the fact who can,
This marvel of an Elephant   35
   Is very like a fan! "

The *Sixth* no sooner had begun
   About the beast to grope,
Than, seizing on the swinging tail
   That fell within his scope,
" I see," quoth he, " the Elephant   40
   Is very like a rope! "

And so these men of Indostan
   Disputed loud and long,
Each in his own opinion   45
   Exceeding stiff and strong,
Though each was partly in the right,
   And all were in the wrong!

THE MORAL:

So, oft in theologic wars,   50
   The disputants, I ween,
Rail on in utter ignorance
   Of what each other mean,
And prate about an Elephant
   Not one of them has seen!

JOHN G. SAXE
From the Hindu

The Enchanted Shirt

1

The King was sick. His cheek was red,
   And his eye was clear and bright;
He ate and drank with a kingly zest,
   And peacefully snored at night.

But he said he was sick, and a king should know,   5
   And doctors came by the score.
They did not cure him. He cut off their heads,
   And sent to the schools for more.

At last two famous doctors came,
   And one was as poor as a rat —   10

He had passed his life in studious toil,
   And never found time to grow fat.

The other had never looked in a book;
   His patients gave him no trouble:
If they recovered, they paid him well;   15
   If they died, their heirs paid double.

Together they looked at the royal tongue,
   As the King on his couch reclined;
In succession they thumped his august chest,
   But no trace of disease could find.   20

The old sage said, " You're as sound as a nut."
   " Hang him up," roared the King in a gale —
In a ten-knot gale of royal rage;
   The other leech grew a shade pale;

But he pensively rubbed his sagacious nose,   25
   And thus his prescription ran:
The King will be well, if he sleeps one night
   In the Shirt of a Happy Man.

2

Wide o'er the realm the couriers rode,
   And fast their horses ran,   30
And many they saw, and to many they spoke,
   But they found no Happy Man.

They found poor men who would fain be rich,
   And rich who thought they were poor;
And men who twisted their waist in stays,   35
   And women that shorthose wore.

They saw two men by the roadside sit,
   And both bemoaned their lot;
For one had buried his wife, he said,
   And the other one had not.   40

At last they came to a village gate,
   A beggar lay whistling there;
He whistled, and sang, and laughed, and rolled
   On the grass in the soft June air.

The weary courtiers paused and looked   45
   At the scamp so blithe and gay;
And one of them said, " Heaven save you, friend!
   You seem to be happy today."

" Oh yes, fair sirs," the rascal laughed,
   And his voice rang free and glad;   50
" An idle man has so much to do
   That he never has time to be sad."

" This is our man," the courier said;
   " Our luck has led us aright.
I will give you a hundred ducats, friend,   55
   For the loan of your shirt tonight."

The merry blackguard lay back on the grass,
   And laughed till his face was black;
" I would do it, God wot," and he roared with the fun,
   " But I haven't a shirt to my back! "   60

3

Each day to the King the reports came in
   Of his unsuccessful spies,

And the sad panorama of human woes
   Passed daily under his eyes.

And he grew ashamed of his useless life,   65
   And his maladies hatched in gloom;
He opened his windows and let the air
   Of the free heaven into his room.

And out he went in the world, and toiled
   In his own appointed way;   70
And the people blessed him, the land was glad,
And the King was well and gay.

JOHN HAY

6
ALL IN
FUN

The Boy Who Laughed at Santa Claus

*Ogden Nash likes to dispose of a subject with a few strange words
and a couple of odd rhymes. Reflecting on " Babies " he writes:*
" A bit of talcum
Is always walcum."
Considering the cow, he concludes:
" The cow is of the bovine ilk;
One end is moo, the other, milk."
*But Ogden Nash also knows how to tell a story, although his way
of telling is as unusual as his rhymes.*

In Baltimore there lived a boy.
He wasn't anybody's joy.
Although his name was Jabez Dawes,
His character was full of flaws.
In school he never led his classes;   5
He hid old ladies' reading glasses;
His mouth was open when he chewed,
And elbows to the table glued.

He stole the milk of hungry kittens,
And walked through doors marked NO ADMITTANCE.   10
He said he acted thus because
There wasn't any Santa Claus.

Another trick that tickled Jabez
Was crying " Boo! " at little babies.
He brushed his teeth, they said in town,   15
Sideways instead of up and down.

Yet people pardoned every sin,
And viewed his antics with a grin,
Till they were told by Jabez Dawes,
" There isn't any Santa Claus! "   20
Deploring how he did behave,
His parents swiftly sought their grave.
They hurried through the portals pearly,
And Jabez left the funeral early.

Like whooping cough, from child to child,   25
He sped to spread the rumor wild:
" Sure as my name is Jabez Dawes
There isn't any Santa Claus! "
Slunk like a weasel or a marten
Through nursery and kindergarten,   30
Whispering low to every tot,
" There isn't any, no there's not! "

The children wept all Christmas Eve
And Jabez chortled up his sleeve.
No infant dared hang up his stocking   35
For fear of Jabez' ribald mocking.
He sprawled on his untidy bed,
Fresh malice dancing in his head,
When presently with scalp a-tingling,
Jabez heard a distant jingling.   40
He heard the crunch of sleigh and hoof
Crisply alighting on the roof.

What good to rise and bar the door?
A shower of soot was on the floor.
What was beheld by Jabez Dawes?   45
The fireplace full of Santa Claus!
Then Jabez fell upon his knees
With cries of " Don't! " and " Pretty please! "
He howled, " I don't know where you read it,
But anyhow, I never said it! "   50

" Jabez," replied the angry saint,
" It isn't I, it's you that ain't.
Although there is a Santa Claus,
There isn't any Jabez Dawes! "
Said Jabez then with impudent vim,   55
" Oh, yes there is; and I am him!
Your magic don't scare *me*, it doesn't " —
And suddenly he found he wasn't!

From grimy feet to grimy locks,
Jabez became a Jack-in-the-box,   60
An ugly toy with springs unsprung,
Forever sticking out his tongue.
The neighbors heard his mournful squeal;
They searched for him, but not with zeal.
No trace was found of Jabez Dawes,   65
Which led to thunderous applause,
And people drank a loving cup
And went and hung their stockings up.

All you who sneer at Santa Claus,
Beware the fate of Jabez Dawes,   70

The saucy boy who mocked the saint.
Donder and Blitzen licked off his paint.

OGDEN NASH

Story

*Dorothy Parker has made many witty comments about modern
life. Behind the humor of her sharp verses there is always a hard
core of common sense. Here, for example, she comments ironically
on the pretended indifference of the girl in the poem.*

" And if he's gone away," said she,
" Good riddance, if you're asking me.
I'm not a one to lie awake
And weep for anybody's sake.
There's better lads than him about!
I'll wear my buckled slippers out
A-dancing till the break of day.
I'm better off with him away!
And if he never come," said she,
" Now what on earth is that to me?
I wouldn't have him back! "
                              I hope
Her mother washed her mouth with soap.

DOROTHY PARKER

Jim

*" Jim," which follows, is a poem which seems to teach a lesson, but
the effect is humorous instead of serious. The story is exaggerated
to the point of burlesque and the tone is mocking. The author,
an English writer of history and biography, included it in a volume
teasingly entitled* Cautionary Tales for Children, *and it makes
sense — in a nonsensical sort of way.*

There was a Boy whose name was Jim;
His Friends were very good to him.
They gave him Tea, and Cakes, and Jam,
And slices of delicious Ham,
And Chocolate with pink inside   5
And little Tricycles to ride,
And read him Stories through and through,
And even took him to the Zoo —
But there it was the dreadful fate
Befell him, which I now relate.   10

You know — at least you ought to know,
For I have often told you so —
That Children never are allowed
To leave their Nurses in a Crowd;
Now this was Jim's especial Foible,   15
He ran away, when he was able,
And on this inauspicious day
He slipped his hand and ran away!

He hadn't gone a yard when — Bang!
With open Jaws, a Lion sprang,   20
And hungrily began to eat
The Boy: beginning at his feet.
Now, just imagine how it feels
When first your toes and then your heels,
And then by gradual degrees,   25
Your shins and ankles, calves and knees,
Are slowly eaten, bit by bit.
No wonder Jim detested it!

No wonder that he shouted " Hi! "
The Honest Keeper heard his cry,   30

Though very fat he almost ran
To help the little gentleman.
" Ponto! " he ordered as he came
(For Ponto was the Lion's name),
" Ponto! " he cried, with angry Frown,   35
" Let go, Sir! Down, Sir! Put it down! "
The Lion made a sudden stop,
He let the Dainty Morsel drop,
And slunk reluctant to his Cage,
Snarling with Disappointed Rage.   40
But when he bent him over Jim,
The Honest Keeper's Eyes were dim.

The Lion having reached his Head,
The Miserable Boy was dead!

When Nurse informed his Parents, they   45
Were more concerned than I can say; —
His Mother, as She dried her eyes,
Said, " Well — it gives me no surprise,
He would not do as he was told! "
His Father, who was self-controlled,   50
Bade all the children round attend
To James's miserable end,
And always keep a-hold of Nurse
For fear of finding something worse.

HILAIRE BELLOC

Captain Reece

W. S. Gilbert will always be remembered as half the team of Gilbert and Sullivan. Some consider him the better half for, although Sullivan wrote delightful music, it was Gilbert who invented the plots and wrote the lyrics for H.M.S. Pinafore, Pirates of Penzance, Patience, The Mikado, Iolanthe, *and their other famous light operas.*

But Gilbert also wrote many humorous poems on his own. The best of them were collected in a volume, the Bab Ballads, *and some of the poems served as plots for several of the operas. " Captain Reece" certainly suggests the captain of the* Pinafore. *Here is the eminent member of the R. N. (Royal Navy), who takes care of his crew almost as lovingly as though they were his children. He supplies them not only with slippers and feather-beds, but with hot-water cans and tobacco (" brown windsor"). He is even thoughtful of the lowly boatswain, or " bosun," the man in charge of the rigging, ropes, and anchor. In fact, his thoughtfulness takes him far — too far — beyond the line of duty.*

Of all the ships upon the blue
No ship contained a better crew
Than that of worthy Captain Reece,
Commanding of *The Mantelpiece*.

He was adored by all his men,   5
For worthy Captain Reece, R.N.,
Did all that lay within him to
Promote the comfort of his crew.

If ever they were dull or sad,
Their captain danced to them like mad,   10
Or told, to make the time pass by,
Droll legends of his infancy.

A feather-bed had every man,
Warm slippers and hot-water can,
Brown windsor from the captain's store,   15
A valet, too, to every four.

New volumes came across the sea
From Mister Mudie's libraree;
The Times and *Saturday Review*
Beguiled the leisure of the crew.   20

Kind-hearted Captain Reece, R.N.,
Was quite devoted to his men;
In point of fact, good Captain Reece
Beatified *The Mantelpiece*.

One summer eve, at half past ten,   25
He said (addressing all his men):
"Come, tell me, please, what can I do
To please and gratify my crew?

" By any reasonable plan
I'll make you happy, if I can;   30
My own convenience count as *nil*;
It is my duty, and I will."

Then up and answered William Lee
(The kindly captain's coxswain he,
A nervous, shy, low-spoken man),   35
He cleared his throat and thus began:

" You have a daughter, Captain Reece,
Ten female cousins and a niece,
A ma, if what I'm told is true,
Six sisters, and an aunt or two.   40

" Now, somehow, sir, it seems to me,
More friendly-like we all should be
If you united of 'em to
Unmarried members of the crew.

" If you'd ameliorate our life,   45
Let each select from them a wife;
And as for nervous me, old pal,
Give me your own enchanting gal! "

Good Captain Reece, that worthy man,
Debated on his coxswain's plan: 50
" I quite agree," he said, " O Bill.
It is my duty and I will.

" My daughter, that enchanting girl,
Has just been promised to an earl,
And all my other familee,   55
To peers of various degree.

" But what are dukes and viscounts to
The happiness of all my crew?
The word I gave you I'll fulfill;
It is my duty, and I will.   60

" As you desire it shall befall,
I'll settle thousands on you all;
And I shall be, despite my hoard,
The only bachelor on board."

The boatswain of *The Mantelpiece*,   65
He blushed and spoke to Captain Reece,
" I beg your honor's leave," he said,
" If you would wish to go and wed,

" I have a widowed mother who
Would be the very thing for you.   70
She long has loved you from afar;
She washes for you, Captain R."

The captain saw the dame that day —
Addressed her in his playful way:
" And did it want a wedding ring?   75
It was a tempting ickle sing!

" Well, well, the chaplain I will seek,
We'll all be married this day week
At yonder church upon the hill;
It is my duty, and I will! "   80

The sisters, cousins, aunts, and niece,
And widowed ma of Captain Reece,
Attended there as they were bid;
It was their duty, and they did.

                                        W. S. GILBERT

Etiquette

In addition to poems which suggested plots for some of Gilbert and Sullivan's light operas, the Bab Ballads contains many others which are full of fun. Sometimes Gilbert's humor and his humanity go hand-in-hand. "Etiquette," for example, is a superbly comic story, and it is also a sly study of character and absurd social customs.

The *Ballyshannon* foundered off the coast of Cariboo,
And down in fathoms many went the captain and the crew;
Down went the owners — greedy men whom hope of gain
    allured:
Oh, dry the starting tear, for they were heavily insured.

Besides the captain and the mate, the owners and the crew,   5
The passengers were also drowned excepting only two:
Young PETER GRAY, who tasted teas for BAKER, CROOP,
    AND CO.,
And SOMERS, who from Eastern shores imported indigo.

These passengers, by reason of their clinging to a mast,
Upon a desert island were eventually cast.   10
They hunted for their meals, as ALEXANDER SELKIRK used,
But they couldn't chat together — they had not been intro-
    duced.

For PETER GRAY and SOMERS too, though certainly in trade,
Were properly particular about the friends they made;   14
And somehow thus they settled it without a word of mouth —
That GRAY should take the northern half, while SOMERS took
    the south.

On PETER's portion oysters grew — a delicacy rare,
But oysters were a delicacy PETER couldn't bear.
On SOMERS' side was turtle, on the shingle lying thick, 19
Which SOMERS couldn't eat, because it always made him sick.

GRAY gnashed his teeth with envy as he saw a mighty store
Of turtle unmolested on his fellow-creature's shore.
The oysters at his feet aside impatiently he shoved,
For turtle and his mother were the only things he loved.

And SOMERS sighed in sorrow as he settled in the south, 25
For the thought of PETER's oysters brought the water to his
    mouth.

He longed to lay him down upon the shelly bed, and stuff:
He had often eaten oysters, but had never had enough.

How they wished an introduction to each other they had had
When on board the *Ballyshannon!* And it drove them nearly
    mad   30
To think how very friendly with each other they might get,
If it wasn't for the arbitrary rule of etiquette!

One day, when out a-hunting for the *mus ridiculus,*
GRAY overheard his fellow-man soliloquizing thus:
" I wonder how the playmates of my youth are getting on,   35
M'CONNELL, S. B. WALTERS, PADDY BYLES, and ROBINSON? "

These simple words made PETER as delighted as could be,
Old chummies at the Charterhouse were ROBINSON and he!
He walked straight up to SOMERS, then he turned extremely
    red,
Hesitated, hummed and hawed a bit, then cleared his throat,
    and said: 40

" I beg your pardon — pray forgive me if I seem too bold,
But you have breathed a name I knew familiarly of old.
You spoke aloud of ROBINSON — I happened to be by.   43
You know him? " " Yes, extremely well." " Allow me, so do I."

It was enough: they felt they could more pleasantly get on,
For (ah, the magic of the fact!) they each knew ROBINSON!
And MR. SOMERS' turtle was at PETER's service quite,
And MR. SOMERS punished PETER's oyster beds all night.

They soon became like brothers from community of wrongs:
They wrote each other little odes and sang each other songs;

204 The Magic Circle

They told each other anecdotes disparaging their wives;   51
On several occasions, too, they saved each other's lives.

They felt quite melancholy when they parted for the night,
And got up in the morning soon as ever it was light;
Each other's pleasant company they reckoned so upon,   55
And all because it happened that they both knew ROBINSON!

They lived for many years on that inhospitable shore,
And day by day they learned to love each other more and
    more.
At last, to their astonishment, on getting up one day,
They saw a frigate anchored in the offing of the bay.   60

To PETER an idea occurred. " Suppose we cross the main?
So good an opportunity may not be found again."
And SOMERS thought a minute, then ejaculated, " Done!
I wonder how my business in the City's getting on."   64

" But stay," said MR. PETER: " when in England, as you know,
I earned a living tasting teas for BAKER, CROOP, AND CO.,
I may be superseded — my employers think me dead! "
" Then come with me," said SOMERS, " and taste indigo in-
    stead."

But all their plans were scattered in a moment when they
    found   69
The vessel was a convict ship from Portland, outward bound;
When a boat came off to fetch them, though they felt it very
    kind,
To go on board they firmly but respectfully declined.

As both the happy settlers roared with laughter at the joke,
They recognized a gentlemanly fellow pulling stroke:

'Twas ROBINSON — a convict, in an unbecoming frock!   75
Condemned to seven years for misappropriating stock!!!

They laughed no more, for SOMERS thought he had been rather
  rash
In knowing one whose friend had misappropriated cash;
And PETER thought a foolish tack he must have gone upon
In making the acquaintance of a friend of ROBINSON.   80

At first they didn't quarrel very openly, I've heard;
They nodded when they met, and now and then exchanged a
  word:
The word grew rare, and rarer still the nodding of the head,
And when they meet each other now, they cut each other
  dead.

To allocate the island they agreed by word of mouth,   85
And PETER takes the north again, and SOMERS takes the south;
And PETER has the oysters, which he hates, in layers thick,
And SOMERS has the turtle — turtle always makes him sick.

W. S. GILBERT

The Walrus and the Carpenter

Almost everyone has read Lewis Carroll's Alice in Wonderland *as
a book, heard it on records and radio, or seen it on the movie or
television screen. It is as lively today as when it was written almost
a hundred years ago, for "Alice" is pure enjoyment as well as a
strange mixture of sense and nonsense. One of the best examples
of Lewis Carroll's logical nonsense is "The Walrus and the Carpenter," a humorous ballad which Tweedledee recites to Alice in*
Through the Looking Glass.

The sun was shining on the sea,
　　Shining with all his might:
He did his very best to make
　　The billows smooth and bright —
And this was odd, because it was   5
　　The middle of the night.

The moon was shining sulkily,
　　Because she thought the sun
Had got no business to be there
　　After the day was done —   10
" It's very rude of him," she said,
　　" To come and spoil the fun."

The sea was wet as wet could be,
　　The sands were dry as dry.
You could not see a cloud, because   15
　　No cloud was in the sky:
No birds were flying overhead —
　　There were no birds to fly.

The Walrus and the Carpenter
　　Were walking close at hand;   20
They wept like anything to see
　　Such quantities of sand;
" If this were only cleared away,"
　　They said, " it *would* be grand."

" If seven maids with seven mops   25
　　Swept it for half a year,
Do you suppose," the Walrus said,
　　" That they could get it clear? "
" I doubt it," said the Carpenter,
　　And shed a bitter tear.   30

" O Oysters, come and walk with us! "
   The Walrus did beseech.
" A pleasant walk, a pleasant talk,
   Along the briny beach:
We cannot do with more than four,   35
   To give a hand to each."

The eldest Oyster looked at him,
   But never a word he said:
The eldest Oyster winked his eye,
   And shook his heavy head —   40
Meaning to say he did not choose
   To leave the oyster bed.

But four young Oysters hurried up,
   All eager for the treat:
Their coats were brushed, their faces washed,   45
   Their shoes were clean and neat —
And this was odd, because, you know,
   They hadn't any feet.

Four other Oysters followed them,
   And yet another four;   50
And thick and fast they came at last,
   And more, and more, and more —
All hopping through the frothy waves,
   And scrambling to the shore.

The Walrus and the Carpentei   55
   Walked on a mile or so,
And then they rested on a rock
   Conveniently low.
And all the little Oysters stood
   And waited in a row.   60

" The time has come," the Walrus said,
    " To talk of many things:
Of shoes — and ships — and sealing-wax —
    Of cabbages — and kings —
And why the sea is boiling hot —   65
    And whether pigs have wings."

" But wait a bit," the Oysters cried,
    " Before we have our chat;
For some of us are out of breath,
    And all of us are fat! "
" No hurry! " said the Carpenter.   70
    They thanked him much for that.

" A loaf of bread," the Walrus said,
　" Is what we chiefly need:
Pepper and vinegar, besides,　　　　　　　75
　Are very good indeed —
Now, if you're ready, Oysters dear,
　We can begin to feed."

" But not on us! " the Oysters cried,
　Turning a little blue.　　　　　　　　80
" After such kindness, that would be
　A dismal thing to do! "
" The night is fine," the Walrus said,
　" Do you admire the view? "

" It was so kind of you to come!　　　85
　And you are very nice! "
The Carpenter said nothing but
　" Cut us another slice:
I wish you were not quite so deaf —
　I've had to ask you twice."　　　　90

" It seems a shame," the Walrus said,
　" To play them such a trick,
After we've brought them out so far,
　And made them trot so quick! "
The Carpenter said nothing but　　　95
　" The butter's spread too thick."

" I weep for you," the Walrus said:
　" I deeply sympathize."
With sobs and tears he sorted out
　Those of the largest size,　　　　　100
Holding his pocket-handkerchief
　Before his streaming eyes.

"O Oysters," said the Carpenter,
  "You've had a pleasant run!
Shall we be trotting home again?"   105
  But answer came there none —
And this was scarcely odd, because
  They'd eaten every one.

LEWIS CARROLL

The Pobble Who Has No Toes

Lewis Carroll and Edward Lear are known as "childhood's mad-cap laureates," authors of the most inspired nonsense ever written. Yet Carroll, in his everyday life, was a university lecturer and mathematical scholar, while Lear was a serious painter whose countless drawings — 10,000 of them were left to one friend alone — are now the pride of museums. It was as a lover of children — he was the youngest of a family of twenty-one brothers and sisters — that Lear invented new words, absurd situations, and creatures as strange and wonderful as the Yonghy-Bhongy-Bo, the Quangle Wangle, the Dong with the Luminous Nose, and the Pobble Who Has No Toes.

The Pobble who has no toes
  Had once as many as we;
When they said, "Some day you may lose them all";
  He replied, "Fish fiddle de-dee!"
And his Aunt Jobiska made him drink   5
Lavender water tinged with pink;
For she said, "The World in general knows
There's nothing so good for a Pobble's toes!"

The Pobble who has no toes,
  Swam across the Bristol Channel;   10

But before he set out he wrapped his nose
   In a piece of scarlet flannel.
For his Aunt Jobiska said, " No harm
Can come to his toes if his nose is warm;
And it's perfectly known that a Pobble's toes   15
Are safe — provided he minds his nose."

The Pobble swam fast and well,
   And when boats or ships came near him,
He tinkledy-binkledy-winked a bell
   So that all the world could hear him.   20
And all the Sailors and Admirals cried,
When they saw him nearing the further side —
" He has gone to fish, for his Aunt Jobiska's
Runcible Cat with crimson whiskers! "

But before he touched the shore —   25
   The shore of the Bristol Channel,
A sea-green Porpoise carried away
   His wrapper of scarlet flannel.
And when he came to observe his feet,
Formerly garnished with toes so neat,   30
His face at once became forlorn
On perceiving that all his toes were gone!

And nobody ever knew,
   From that dark day to the present,
Whoso had taken the Pobble's toes,   35
   In a manner so far from pleasant.
Whether the shrimps or crawfish gray,
Or crafty Mermaids stole them away,
Nobody knew; and nobody knows
How the Pobble was robbed of his twice five toes!   40

The Pobble who has no toes
  Was placed in a friendly Bark,
And they rowed him back, and carried him up
  To his Aunt Jobiska's Park.
And she made him a feast, at his earnest wish,   45
Of eggs and buttercups fried with fish;
And she said, " It's a fact the whole world knows,
That Pobbles are happier without their toes."

EDWARD LEAR

The Dumb Wife Cured

There was a bonny blade
Had wed a country maid,
And safely conducted her
Home, home, home.
She was neat in every part,   5
And she pleased him from the start,
But, ah and alas, she was
Dumb, dumb, dumb.

She was bright as the day,
And as brisk as the May,   10
And as round and as plump as a
Plum, plum, plum;
But still the silly swain
Could do nothing but complain
Because that his wife was   15
Dumb, dumb, dumb.

She could brew, she could bake,
She could sew, and she could make,

She could sweep the house with a
Broom, broom, broom;   20
She could wash and she could wring,
Could do any kind of thing,
But, ah, alas, she was
Dumb, dumb, dumb.

To the doctor then he went   25
For to give himself content,
And to cure his wife of the
Mum, mum, mum:
" Oh, it is the easiest part
That belongs unto my art,   30
For to make a woman speak that is
Dumb, dumb, dumb."

To the doctor he did her bring
And he cut her chattering string,
And at liberty he set her   35
Tongue, tongue, tongue;
Her tongue began to walk,
And she began to talk
As though she had never been
Dumb, dumb, dumb.   40

Her faculty she found
And she filled the house with sound,
And she rattled in his ears like a
Drum, drum, drum:
She bred a deal of strife,   45
Made him weary of his life,
He'd give anything again she was
Dumb, dumb, dumb.

To the doctor then he goes
And thus he vents his woes,   50
" Oh, doctor, you've me un-
Done, done, done,
For my wife she's turned a scold,
And her tongue can never hold,
I'd give any kind of thing she was   55
Dumb, dumb, dumb."

" When I did undertake
To make thy wife to speak,
It was a thing eas-i-ly
Done, done, done,   60
But 'tis past the art of man,
Let him do whate'er he can
For to make a scolding woman hold her
Tongue, tongue, tongue."

AUTHOR UNKNOWN

Elegy on the Death of a Mad Dog

Good people all, of every sort,
  Give ear unto my song;
And if you find it wondrous short, —
  It cannot hold you long.

In Islington there was a man,   5
  Of whom the world might say,
That still a godly race he ran, —
  Whene'er he went to pray.

A kind and gentle heart he had,
  To comfort friends and foes;   10
The naked every day he clad, —
  When he put on his clothes.

And in that town a dog was found,
  As many dogs there be,
Both mongrel, puppy, whelp, and hound,   15
  And curs of low degree.

This dog and man at first were friends;
  But when a pique began,
The dog, to gain some private ends,
  Went mad, and bit the man.   20

Around from all the neighboring streets,
  The wondering neighbors ran,
And swore the dog had lost his wits,
  To bite so good a man.

The wound it seemed both sore and sad   25
  To every Christian eye;
And while they swore the dog was mad,
  They swore the man would die.

But soon a wonder came to light,
  That showed the rogues they lied;   30
The man recovered of the bite,
  The dog it was that died.

OLIVER GOLDSMITH

The Aged Stranger

" I was with Grant," the stranger said.
  Said the farmer: " Say no more,
But rest thee here at my cottage porch,
  For thy feet are weary and sore."

" I was with Grant — " the stranger said;   5
  Said the farmer. " Nay, no more, —
I prithee sit at my frugal board,
  And eat of my humble store.

" How fares my boy, — my soldier boy,
  Of the old Ninth Army Corps?   10
I warrant he bore him gallantly
  In the smoke and the battle's roar! "

" I know him not," said the aged man,
  " And, as I remarked before,
I was with Grant — " " Nay, nay, I know,"   15
  Said the farmer, " say no more.

" He fell in battle, — I see, alas!
   Thou'dst smooth these tidings o'er, —
Nay, speak the truth, whatever it be,
   Though it rend my bosom's core.   20

" How fell he? — with his face to the foe,
   Upholding the flag he bore?
Oh, say not that my boy disgraced
   The uniform that he wore! "

" I cannot tell," said the aged man,   25
   " And should have remarked before,
That I was with Grant — in Illinois —
   Some three years before the war."

Then the farmer spake him never a word,
   But beat with his fist full sore   30
That aged man, who had worked for Grant
   Some three years before the war.

                     BRET HARTE

The King and the Clown

*The story of " The King and the Clown " is as old as its subjects:
life and death. It appears — and reappears — in every land and in
every language. The rhymed treatment which follows is the most
recent version; this is the first time it has ever been printed.*

There once was a monarch, a pompous old Persian,
   Whose frown was a threat and his nod a command.
Yet, there at his side, as a needed diversion,
   A quick-witted jester was always on hand.

For a while there were smiles, for a while there was laughter;
  Then, one evil day, the king's petulance spoke: 6
"There's been too much fooling. You're finished! And after
  You're dead you'll discover that life is no joke.

"I might have you tortured, then add something crueler:
  Hung up by your toenails or torn by a cur;   10
But I am a merry and merciful ruler,
  And so you may choose any death you prefer."

The clown paled and wept. Then, abrupt, he stopped crying
  And grinned at the monarch. "Don't fly in a rage,
But, since I can choose my own method of dying,   15
  I choose (and I thank you) to die of old age."

FROM THE PERSIAN
Adapted by Michael Lewis

The Twins

In form and feature, face and limb,
  I grew so like my brother,
That folks got taking me for him,
  And each for one another.

It puzzled all our kith and kin,   5
   It reached a fearful pitch;
For one of us was born a twin,
   Yet not a soul knew which.

One day, to make the matter worse,
   Before our names were fixed,   10
As we were being washed by nurse,
   We got completely mixed;
And thus, you see, by fate's decree,
   Or rather nurse's whim,
My brother John got christened me,   15
   And I got christened him.

This fatal likeness even dogged
   My footsteps when at school,
And I was always getting flogged,
   For John turned out a fool.   20
I put this question, fruitlessly,
   To everyone I knew,
" What *would* you do, if you were me,
   To prove that you were *you?* "

Our close resemblance turned the tide   25
   Of my domestic life,
For somehow, my intended bride
   Became my brother's wife.
In fact, year after year the same
   Absurd mistakes went on,   30
And when I died, the neighbors came
   And buried brother John.

HENRY SAMBROOKE LEIGH

How to Tell Wild Animals

If ever you should go by chance
   To jungles in the East;
And if there should to you advance
   A large and tawny beast,
If he roars at you as you're dyin'   5
You'll know it is the Asian Lion.

Or if sometime when roaming round,
   A noble wild beast greets you,
With black stripes on a yellow ground,
   Just notice if he eats you.   10
This simple rule may help you learn
The Bengal Tiger to discern.

If strolling forth, a beast you view,
   Whose hide with spots is peppered,
As soon as he has lept on you,   15
   You'll know it is the Leopard.
'Twill do no good to roar with pain,
He'll only lep and lep again.

If when you're walking round your yard,
   You meet a creature there,   20
Who hugs you very, very hard,
   Be sure it is the Bear.
If you have any doubt, I guess
He'll give you just one more caress.

Though to distinguish beasts of prey   25
   A novice might nonplus,
The Crocodiles you always may

Tell from Hyenas thus:
Hyenas come with merry smiles;
But if they weep, they're Crocodiles.   30

The true Chameleon is small,
    A lizard sort of thing;
He hasn't any ears at all,
    And not a single wing.
If there is nothing on the tree,   35
'Tis the Chameleon you see.

CAROLYN WELLS

Old-Fashioned Love

He struggled to kiss her. She struggled the same
    To prevent him so bold and undaunted;
But, as smitten by lightning, he heard her exclaim,
    " Avaunt, Sir! " and off he avaunted.

Then he meekly approached, and sat down at her feet,
    Praying loud, as before he had ranted,
That she would forgive him, and try to be sweet,
    And said " Can't you? " The dear girl recanted.

Then softly he whispered, " How could you do so?
    I certainly thought I was jilted;
But come thou with me, to the parson we'll go.
    Say, wilt thou, my dear? " And she wilted.

AUTHOR UNKNOWN

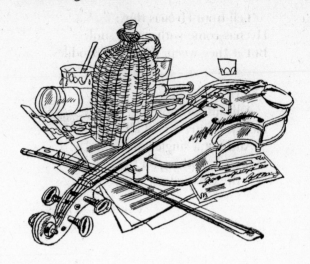

Ten Brothers

All of us can remember verses that add and subtract; they range all the way from childhood's "Ten Little Indians" to the Christmas carol, "I Will Sing You One-O." Every country has its own kind of "counting" poems, and the following one from Russia is among the jolliest.

We used to be ten brothers,
    Our business, it was wine.
One of us liked his trade too well —
    Now we're only nine.
Oh! Jascha, bring your fiddle   5
    And Sascha, take the air;
Come and play a little
    In the middle of the square.

We used to be nine brothers,
    Our business, it was freight.   10

One of us fell beneath a load —
   Now we're only eight.
Oh! Jascha, etc.

We used to be eight brothers,
   Our business was uneven.   15
One of us picked a lawyer's purse —
   Now we're only seven.
Oh! Jascha, etc.

We used to be seven brothers,
   Our business was with bricks.   20
One of us made a slight mistake —
   Now we're only six.
Oh! Jascha, etc.

We used to be six brothers,
   Our business did not thrive.   25
One of us found a wealthy widow —
   Now we're only five.
Oh! Jascha, etc.

We used to be five brothers,
   Our country went to war.   30
One of us traded at the front —
   Now we're only four.
Oh! Jascha, etc.

We used to be four brothers,
   Our business was at sea.   35
One of us bought himself a ship —
   Now we're only three.
Oh! Jascha, etc.

We used to be three brothers,
   Our business, it was glue.   40
One of us fell into the vat —
   Now we're only two.
Oh! Jascha, etc.

We used to be two brothers,
   We never could agree.   45
Our business was too small for both —
   Now there's only me.
Oh! Jascha, etc.

I am the last of the brothers,
   Our business died away.   50
And since there's never enough to eat,
   I perish every day.
Oh! Jascha, bring your fiddle
   And Sascha, take the air;
Come and play a little   55
   In the middle of the square.

FROM THE YIDDISH
Adapted by Louis Untermeyer

Four Ruthless Rhymes

Billy

Billy, in one of his nice new sashes,
Fell in the grate and was burned to ashes.
Now, although the room grows chilly,
I haven't the heart to poke up Billy.

Nurse

Making toast at the fireside,   5
Nurse fell in the grate and died.
But, what makes it ten times worse,
All the toast was burned with Nurse.

Mr. Jones

" There's been an accident," they said.
" Your servant's cut in half; he's dead."   10
" Too bad," said Mr. Jones, " but please
Send me the half that's got my keys."

Aunt Eliza

In the drinking well
    Which the plumber built her,
Aunt Eliza fell.   15
    We must buy a filter.

HARRY   GRAHAM

The Society upon the Stanislow

*Like Mark Twain, Bret Harte visited the West when it was a
rugged frontier. In the small towns where gold miners and ranch-
men gathered they sometimes tried to imitate the refined East but
rarely succeeded. In this poem Harte tells of a learned society in
such a town, which has gathered together to discuss scientific mat-
ters. The meeting ends in a somewhat ungentlemanly way!*

I reside at Table Mountain, and my name is Truthful James:
I am not up to small deceit or any sinful games;

And I'll tell in simple language what I know about the
    row
That broke up our Society upon the Stanislow.

Now, nothing could be finer, or more beautiful to see,   5
Than the first six months' proceedings of that same society;
    Till Brown of Calaveras brought a lot of fossil bones
    That he found within a tunnel near the tenement of
        Jones.

Then Brown he read a paper, and he reconstructed there,   9
From those same bones, an animal that was extremely rare;
    And Jones then asked the Chair for a suspension of the
        rules,
    Till he could prove that those same bones was one of his
        lost mules.

Then Brown he smiled a bitter smile, and said he was at fault;
It seemed he had been trespassing on Jones's family vault;
    He was a most sarcastic man, this quiet Mr. Brown,   15
    And on several occasions he had cleaned out the town.

Now I hold it is not decent for a scientific gent
To say another is an ass — at least, to all intent;
    Nor should the individual who happens to be meant
    Reply by heaving rocks at him to any great extent.   20

Then Abner Dean of Angel's raised a point of order, when
A chunk of old red sandstone took him in the abdomen;
    And he smiled a kind of sickly smile, and curled up on the
        floor,
    And the subsequent proceedings interested him no more.

For in less time than I write it, every member did engage   25
In a warfare with the remnants of a paleozoic age;
    And the way they heaved those fossils in their anger was
        a sin,
    Till the skull of an old mammoth caved the head of
        Thompson in.

And this is all I have to say of these improper games,
For I live at Table Mountain and my name is Truthful James,
    And I've told in simple language what I know about the
        row   31
    That broke up our Society upon the Stanislow.

BRET HARTE

The Cremation of Sam McGee

*" The Shooting of Dan McGrew " by Robert W. Service appears
on page 51. The poem which follows is also by Service, but though
the titles may seem similar the poems are quite different in effect.
The first is grim, while the second is gay. Told with the same
strong beat and bouncing rhymes, " The Cremation of Sam
McGee " has become a part of our native folklore; it has been told
often before as a tall tale and as a joke, but never better, never
more vivaciously than here.*

    There are strange things done in the midnight sun
        By the men who moil for gold;
    The Arctic trails have their secret tales
        That would make your blood run cold;
    The Northern Lights have seen queer sights,   5
        But the queerest they ever did see
    Was that night on the marge of Lake Lebarge
        I cremated Sam McGee.

Now Sam McGee was from Tennessee, where the cotton
blooms and blows.
Why he left his home in the South to roam 'round the Pole,
God only knows.   10
He was always cold, but the land of gold seemed to hold him
like a spell;
Though he'd often say in his homely way that "he'd sooner
live in hell."

On a Christmas Day we were mushing our way over the Daw-
son trail.
Talk of your cold! through the parka's fold it stabbed like a
driven nail.
If our eyes we'd close, then the lashes froze till sometimes we
couldn't see;   15
It wasn't much fun, but the only one to whimper was Sam
McGee.

And that very night, as we lay packed tight in our robes be-
neath the snow,
And the dogs were fed, and the stars o'erhead were dancing
heel and toe,
He turned to me, and "Cap," says he, "I'll cash in this trip,
I guess;   19
And if I do, I'm asking that you won't refuse my last request."

Well, he seemed so low that I couldn't say no; then he says
with a sort of moan:
"It's the cursèd cold, and it's got right hold till I'm chilled
clean through to the bone.
Yet 'tain't being dead — it's my awful dread of the icy grave
that pains;
So I want you to swear that, foul or fair, you'll cremate my
last remains."

A pal's last need is a thing to heed, so I swore I would not fail;
And we started on at the streak of dawn; but God! he looked
    ghastly pale.   26
He crouched on the sleigh, and he raved all day of his home
    in Tennessee;
And before nightfall a corpse was all that was left of Sam
    McGee.

There wasn't a breath in that land of death, and I hurried,
    horror-driven,
With a corpse half hid that I couldn't get rid, because of a
    promise given;   30
It was lashed to the sleigh, and it seemed to say: "You may
    tax your brawn and brains,
But you promised true, and it's up to you to cremate those
    last remains."

Now a promise made is a debt unpaid, and the trail has its
    own stern code.
In the days to come, though my lips were dumb, in my heart
    how I cursed that load.
In the long, long night, by the lone firelight, while the huskies,
    round in a ring,   35
Howled out their woes to the homeless snows — O God! how
    I loathed the thing.

And every day that quiet clay seemed to heavy and heavier
    grow;
And on I went, though the dogs were spent and the grub was
    getting low;
The trail was bad, and I felt half mad, but I swore I would
    not give in;
And I'd often sing to the hateful thing, and it hearkened with
    a grin.   40

Till I came to the marge of Lake Lebarge, and a derelict there
  lay;
It was jammed in the ice, but I saw in a trice it was called the
  Alice May.
And I looked at it, and I thought a bit, and I looked at my
  frozen chum;
Then " Here," said I, with a sudden cry, " is my cre-ma-tor-
  eum."

Some planks I tore from the cabin floor, and I lit the boiler
  fire;   45
Some coal I found that was lying around, and I heaped the
  fuel higher;
The flames just soared, and the furnace roared — such a blaze
  you seldom see;
And I burrowed a hole in the glowing coal, and I stuffed in
  Sam McGee.

Then I made a hike, for I didn't like to hear him sizzle so;
And the heavens scowled, and the huskies howled, and the
  wind began to blow.   50
It was icy cold, but the hot sweat rolled down my cheeks, and
  I don't know why;
And the greasy smoke in an inky cloak went streaking down
  the sky.

I do not know how long in the snow I wrestled with grisly
  fear;
But the stars came out and they danced about ere again I
  ventured near;
I was sick with dread, but I bravely said: " I'll just take a peep
  inside.   55
I guess he's cooked, and it's time I looked " . . . then the
  door I opened wide.

And there sat Sam, looking cool and calm, in the heart of the
    furnace roar;
And he wore a smile you could see a mile, and he said: " Please
    close that door.
It's fine in here, but I greatly fear you'll let in the cold and
    storm —
Since I left Plumtree, down in Tennessee, it's the first time
    I've been warm."   60

There are strange things done in the midnight sun
   By the men who moil for gold;
The Arctic trails have their secret tales
   That would make your blood run cold;
The Northern Lights have seen queer sights,   65
   But the queerest they ever did see
Was that night on the marge of Lake Lebarge
   I cremated Sam McGee.

ROBERT W. SERVICE

7
BALLADS OF
THE OLD DAYS

Lord Randall

*Nobody knows who made the first ballad nor when it was made.
Ballads, or stories in song, were heard in the Scandinavian countries as early as the twelfth century; the Anglo-Saxons of ancient
England and the Celts in Scotland and Ireland delighted in them.
Most of the ballads traveled across the Atlantic, and were there
adapted to new situations and transformed into American folk
songs, from the lumberjack songs of Maine to the "lonesome
tunes" of Kentucky.*

*These old popular ballads belonged to the masses, to the unedu-
cated folk; they were made up, enjoyed, and remembered long before they were written down. Every singer made his own changes,
supplied new incidents and added lines of his own. "Lord Randall," one of the most popular old English ballads, appears in
scores of versions.*

" Where have you been all the day, Randall, my son?
Where have been all the day, my pretty one? "
" I've been to my sweetheart's, mother;
Oh, make my bed soon,
For I'm sick to my heart and I fain would lie down."   5

" What did she feed you, Randall, my son?
What did she feed you, my pretty one? "

"Eels boiled in broth, mother;
Oh, make my bed soon,
For I'm sick to my heart and I fain would lie down."　　　10

"Oh, I fear you are poisoned, Randall, my son,
I fear you are poisoned, my pretty one."
"Oh, yes, I am poisoned, mother;
Make my bed soon,
For I'm sick to my heart and I fain would lie down."　　　15

"What will you leave your mother, Randall, my son?
What will you leave your mother, my pretty one?"
"A dead son to bury, mother;
Oh, make my bed soon,
For I'm sick to my heart and I fain would lie down."　　　20

"What will you leave your sweetheart, Randall, my son?
What will you leave your sweetheart, my pretty one?"
"A rope to hang her, mother;
Oh, make my bed soon,
For I'm sick to my heart and I fain would lie down."

AUTHOR UNKNOWN

The Douglas Tragedy

Like many of the old ballads, "The Douglas Tragedy" is a wild and gory tale. Its atmosphere is one of terror; the heroine is torn between loyalty to her father and devotion to her lover. In Selkirkshire, England, seven large stones are still shown to visitors, who are told that the stones represent the seven brothers who were slain. The Douglas rivulet is declared to be the very stream at which the lovers alighted to drink, and it is even said that the dark color of the stream is due to Lord William's blood which stained "the spring that ran so clear."

" Rise up, rise up, Lord Douglas! " she says,
  " And put on your armor so bright;
Let it ne'er be said that a daughter of ours
  Was married to a lord under night.

" Rise up, rise up, my seven bold sons,   5
  And put on your armor so bright;
And take better care of your youngest sister.
  For your eldest's away this night! "

Lady Margaret was on a milk-white steed,
  Lord William was on a gray,   10
A buglet-horn hung down by his side,
  And swiftly they rode away.

Lord William looked over his left shoulder
  To see what he could see,
And there he spied her seven bold brothers   15
  Come riding over the lea.

" Light down, light down, Lady Margaret," he said,
  " And hold my steed in your hand,
Until that against your seven bold brothers,
  And your father, I make a stand."   20

O, there she stood, and bitter she stood,
  And never shed one tear,
Until she saw her brothers fall,
  And her father who loved her so dear.

" O hold your hand, Lord William! " she said,   25
  " For your strokes are deep and sore;
Though lovers I can get many a one,
  A father I can never get more."

O she's taken off her handkerchief,
   It was of the holland so fine,   30
And aye she dressed her father's wounds;
   His blood ran down like wine.

" O choose, O choose, Lady Margaret,
   Will ye go with me, or bide? "
" I'll go, I'll go, Lord William," she said.   35
   " Ye've left me no other guide."

He lifted her up on her milk-white steed,
   And mounted his dapple-gray,
With his buglet-horn hung down by his side,
   And slowly they rode away.   40

O they rode on, and on they rode,
   And all by the light of the moon,
Until they came to a wan water,
   And there they lighted down.

They lighted down to take a drink   45
   Of the spring that ran so clear,
But down the stream ran his red heart's blood,
   And she began to fear.

" Hold up, hold up, Lord William," she said,
   " I fear me you are slain! "   50
" 'Tis but the shadow of my scarlet cloak
   That shines in the water so plain."

O they rode on, and on they rode,
   And all by the light of the moon,
Until they saw his mother's hall,   55
   And there they lighted down.

" Get up, get up, lady mother," he says,
　" Get up, and let in your son!
Open the door, lady mother," he says,
　" For this night my fair lady I've won!　　60

" Now make my bed, lady mother," he says,
　" O make it wide and deep,
And lay Lady Margaret close at my back,
　And the sounder will I sleep! "

Lord William was dead long ere midnight,　　65
　Lady Margaret long ere day;
And all true lovers that go together
　May they have more luck than they!

Lord William was buried in Mary's Kirk,
　Lady Margaret in Mary's Choir;　　70
And out of her grave grew a bonny red rose,
　And out of the knight's a briar.

The briar twined about the rose,
　And the rose clung to the briar,
And so they grew ever closer together,　　75
　As all true lovers desire.

AUTHOR UNKNOWN

Edward, Edward

The old ballads are full of sudden, cruel deeds. In the ballad, action begins immediately; there is no introduction and practically no explanation. Everything is speeded up; the setting, the dialogue, and the ending are part of one rapid, uninterrupted progress. In " Ed-

*ward, Edward" the tale begins with a mother questioning her son.
She notices blood dripping from his sword, and he hesitates to tell
the truth about it. First he says that he killed his hawk; then he
answers that it is his horse which has been killed. Finally he blurts
out the truth, but the full horror is not revealed until the last
stanza, with the last terrible reply.*

" Why does your sword so drip with blood,
    Edward, Edward?
Why does your sword so drip with blood,
  And why so sad are ye, O? "
" O I have killed my hawk so good,   5
    Mother, mother,
O I have killed my hawk so good
  And I had no more but he, O."

" Your hawk's blood was never so red,
    Edward, Edward,   10
Your hawk's blood was never so red,
  My dear son, I tell thee, O."
" O I have killed my red-roan steed,
    Mother, mother,
O I have killed my red-roan steed,   15
  That was so fair and free, O."

" Your steed was old and your stable's filled,
    Edward, Edward,
Your steed was old and your stable's filled,
  Now say what may it be, O."   20
" It was my father that I killed,
    Mother, mother,
It was my father that I killed,
  Alas, and woe is me, O."

" What penance will ye do for that,   25
    Edward, Edward?
What penance will ye do for that,
  My dear son, now tell me, O? "
" I'll set my feet in yonder boat,
    Mother, mother,   30
I'll set my feet in yonder boat,
  And I'll fare across the sea, O."

" What will ye do with your towers and hall,
    Edward, Edward?
What will ye do with your towers and hall,   35
  That are so fair to see, O? "
" I'll let them stand till down they fall,
    Mother, mother,
I'll let them stand till down they fall,
  For here nevermore may I be, O."   40

" What will ye leave to your babes and your wife,
    Edward, Edward?
What will ye leave to your babes and your wife,
  When ye go over the sea, O? "
" The world's room — let them beg through life,   45
    Mother, mother,
The world's room — let them beg through life,
  For them nevermore will I see, O."

" And what will ye leave to your own mother dear,
    Edward, Edward?   50
And what will ye leave to your own mother dear,
  My dear son, now tell me, O? "

"The curse of Hell from me shall ye bear,
     Mother, mother,
The curse of Hell from me shall ye bear: 55
     Such counsel ye gave to me, O!"

AUTHOR UNKNOWN

True Thomas

*This ballad has a genuine historic origin. Thomas of Erceldowne,
known as Thomas the Rhymer, was not only a poet but a prophet
who lived in the twelfth or thirteenth century. Two or three hundred years after he died, an unknown minstrel composed a ballad
about the poet who was called True Thomas because he could not
lie. The tale relates how a mortal singer is enticed by a fairy lady;
its theme has long been a favorite of composers and poets. In the
early nineteenth century, the poet John Keats added his own
charm to the old magic, and turned the ballad into the exquisite
poetry of " La Belle Dame sans Merci," on page 46.*

True Thomas lay on Huntlie bank;
     A marvel he did see;
For there he saw a lady bright,
     Come riding down by the Eildon tree.

Her skirt was of the grass-green silk   5
     Her cloak of the velvet fine;
On every lock of her horse's mane
     Hung fifty silver bells and nine.

True Thomas he pulled off his cap,
     And bowed low down on his knee;   10
"All hail, thou mighty Queen of Heaven!
     For thy peer on earth could never be."

" O no, O no, Thomas," she said,
   That name does not belong to me;
" I'm but the Queen of fair Elfland,   15
   That hither am come to visit thee.

" Walk and talk, Thomas," she said,
   " Walk and talk along with me;
And if ye dare to kiss my lips,
   Sure of your body I will be! "   20

" If it be good, or if it be bad,
   That fate shall never frighten me."
Then he has kissed her on the lips,
   All underneath the Eildon tree.

" Now ye must go with me," she said,   25
   " True Thomas, ye must go with me;
And ye must serve me seven years,
   Through weal or woe, as may chance to be."

She's mounted on her milk-white steed,
   She's taken True Thomas up behind;   30
And aye, when'er her bridle rang,
   The steed flew swifter than the wind.

O they rode on, and farther on,
   The steed flew swifter than the wind;
Until they reached a desert wide,   35
   And living land was left behind.

" Light down, light down now, Thomas," she said,
   " And lean your head upon my knee;
Light down, and rest a little space,
   And I will show you marvels three.   40

" O see ye not yon narrow road,
  So thick beset with thorns and briars?
That is the path of righteousness,
  Though after it but few enquires.

" And see ye not yon broad, broad road,   45
  That stretches far and wide and even?
That is the path of wickedness,
  Though some may call it the road to heaven.

" And see ye not yon bonny road,
  That winds about the green hillside?   50
That is the way to fair Elfland,
  Where you and I this night must bide.

" But, Thomas, ye shall hold your tongue,
  Whatever ye may hear or see;
For if ye speak word in Elfinland,   55
  Ye'll ne'er win back to your own countree! "

O they rode on, and farther on;
  They waded through rivers above the knee,
And they saw neither sun or moon,
  But they heard the roaring of the sea.   60

It was dark, dark night; there was no starlight;
  They waded through red blood to the knee;
For all the blood that's shed on earth,
  Runs through the springs o' that countree.

At last they came to a garden green,   65
  And she pulled an apple from on high —
" Take this for thy wages, True Thomas;
  It will give thee the tongue that can never lie! "

" My tongue is my own," True Thomas he said,
  " A goodly gift ye would give to me!   70
I never could hope to buy or sell
  At fair or tryst where I may be.

" I never could speak to prince or peer,
  Nor ask of grace from fair lady."
" Now hold thy peace! " the lady said,   75
  " For as I say, so must it be."

He has gotten a coat of the even cloth,
  And a pair of shoes of the velvet green;
And till seven years were gone and past,
  True Thomas on earth was never seen.

AUTHOR UNKNOWN

Robin Hood and the Tanner

Songs and stories about Robin Hood were popular in England as early as the fourteenth century. One of them, " A Gest of Robyn Hode," was compiled at the time of the discovery of America. Everyone knew and loved the story of the man who became an outlaw, lived in the greenwood, robbed wealthy nobles, but was loyal to his king and gave to the poor what he took from the rich. The ballads picture him as a man of dignity, grace, liberality, and humor. This last quality is especially revealed in the following ballad.

In Nottingham there lives a jolly tanner,
  His name is Arthur a Bland;
There is ne'er a squire in Nottinghamshire
  Dare bid bold Arthur stand.

With a long pike-staff upon his shoulder,   5
  So well he can clear his way;

By two and by three he makes them to flee,
   For they have no desire to stay.

And as he went forth, one summer's morning,
   Into the forest of merry Sherwood,   10
In view the red deer that range here and there,
   He met with bold Robin Hood.

As soon as bold Robin Hood did him espy,
   He thought some sport he would make;
Therefore out of hand he bid him to stand,   15
   And thus to him he spake:

" Why, what art thou, thou bold fellow,
   That ranges so boldly here?
In sooth, to be brief, thou look'st like a thief,
   That comes to steal our king's deer.   20

" For I am a keeper in this forest;
   The king puts me in trust
To look to his deer, that range here and there,
   Therefore stay thee I must."

" If thou beest a keeper in this forest,   25
   And hast such a great command,
Yet thou must have more helpers in arms,
   Before thou make me to stand."

" Nay, I ask no more helpers in arms,
   Or any that I do need;   30
But I have a staff of another oak graff,
   I know it will do the deed."

Then Robin Hood he unbuckled his belt,
   He laid down his bow so long;
He took up a staff of another oak graff,   35
   That was both stiff and strong.

" I'll yield to thy weapon," said jolly Robin,
   " Since thou wilt not yield to mine;
For I have a staff of another oak graff,
   Not half a foot longer then thine.   40

" But let me measure," said jolly Robin,
   " Before we begin our fray;
For I'll not have mine to be longer then thine,
   For that will be called foul play."

" I pass not for length," bold Arthur replied,   45
   " My staff is of oak so free;
Eight foot and a half, it will knock down a calf,
   And I hope it will knock down thee."

Then Robin Hood could no longer forbear;
   He gave him such a knock,   50
Quickly and soon the blood came down,
   Before it was ten o'clock.

Then Arthur he soon recovered himself,
   And gave him such a knock on the crown,
That on every hair of bold Robin Hood's head,   55
   The blood came trickling down.

Then Robin Hood raged like a wild boar,
   As soon as he saw his own blood;
But Bland was in haste, he laid on so fast,
   As though he had been stacking of wood.   60

And about, and about, and about they went,
    Like two wild boars in a chase;
Striving to aim each other to maim
    Leg, arm, or any other place.

And knock for knock they lustily dealt,   65
    Which held for two hours and more;
That all the wood rang at every bang,
    They plied their work so sore.

" Hold thy hand, hold thy hand." said Robin Hood,
    " And let our quarrel fall;   70
For here we may thresh our bones into mesh,
    And get no coin at all.

" And in the forest of merry Sherwood
    Hereafter thou shalt be free."   74
" God-a-mercy for naught, my freedom I bought,
    I may thank my good staff, not thee! "

" What tradesman art thou? " said jolly Robin,
    " Good fellow, I prithee me show:
And also me tell in what place thou dost dwell,
    For both these fain would I know."   80

" I am a tanner," bold Arthur replied,
    " In Nottingham long have I wrought;
And if thou come there, I vow and do swear
    I will tan thy hide for naught."

" God-a-mercy, good fellow," said jolly Robin,   85
    " Since thou art so kind to me;
And if thou wilt tan my hide for naught.
    I will do as much for thee.

" But if thou will forsake thy tanner's trade,
   And live in the greenwood with me,   90
My name's Robin Hood, I swear by the rood
   I will give thee both gold and fee."

" If thou be Robin Hood," bold Arthur replied,
   " As I think well thou art,
Then here's my hand, my name's Arthur a Bland,
   We two will never depart."   96

" But tell me, O tell me, where is Little John?
   Of him fain would I hear;
For we are allied by the mother's side,
   And he is my kinsman near."   100

Then Robin Hood blew on the bugle horn,
   He blew full loud and shrill,
But quickly anon appeared Little John,
   Come tripping down a green hill.

" O what is the matter? " then said Little John,   105
   " Master, I pray you tell.
Why do you stand with your staff in your hand?
   I fear all is not well."

" O man, I do stand, and he makes me to stand,
   The tanner that stands thee beside;   110
He is a bonny blade, and master of his trade,
   For soundly he hath tanned my hide."

" He is to be commended," then said Little John,
   " If such a feat he can do;
If he be so stout, we will have a bout,   115
   And he shall tan my hide, too."

" Hold thy hand, hold thy hand," said Robin Hood,
   " For as I do understand,
He's a yeoman good, and of thine own blood,
   For his name is Arthur a Bland."   120

Then Little John threw his staff away,
   As far as he could it fling,
And ran out of hand to Arthur a Bland,
   And about his neck did cling.

Then Robin Hood took them both by the hand,
   And danced round about the oak tree;   126
" For three merry men, and three merry men,
   And three merry men we be!

" And ever hereafter, as long as I live,
   We three will be all one;   130
The wood shall ring, and the old wife sing,
   Of Robin Hood, Arthur, and John."

AUTHOR UNKNOWN

The Golden Glove

A wealthy young squire of Tamworth we hear,
He courted a nobleman's daughter so fair;
To marry this lady it was his intent,
All friends and relations gave gladly consent.

The time was appointed for their wedding day,   5
A young farmer chosen to give her away;
As soon as the farmer this lady did spy,
He inflamed her heart; " Oh my heart! " she did cry.

She turned from the squire, but nothing she said;
Instead of being married she took to her bed.   10
The thought of the farmer ran sore in her mind;
A way to secure him she quickly did find.

Coat, waistcoat, and breeches she then did put on,
And a-hunting she went with her dog and her gun;
She hunted around where the farmer did dwell,   15
Because in her heart she did love him full well.

She oftentimes fired, but nothing she killed,
At length the young farmer came into the field;
And as to discourse with him was her intent,
With her dog and her gun to meet him she went.   20

" I thought you had been at the wedding," she cried,
" To wait on the squire, and give him his bride."
" No, sir," said the farmer, " if the truth I may tell,
I'll not give her away, for I love her too well."

" Suppose that the lady should grant you her love?   25
You know that the squire your rival would prove."
" Why, then," says the farmer, " with sword-blade in hand,
By honor I'll gain her when she shall command."

It pleased the lady to find him so bold;
She gave him a glove that was flowered with gold,   30
And she told him she found it when coming along,
As she was a-hunting with dog and with gun.

The lady went home with a heart full of love,
And she gave out a notice that she'd lost a glove;
And said, " Who has found it, and brings it to me,   35
Whoever he is, he my husband shall be."

The farmer was pleased when he heard of the news,
With heart full of joy to the lady he goes.
" Dear honored lady, I've picked up your glove,
And hope you'll be pleased to grant me your love."   40

" It already is granted, and I'll be your bride;
I love the sweet breath of a farmer," she cried,
" I'll be mistress of dairy, and milking the cow,
While my jolly brisk farmer sings sweet at the plow."

And when she was married she told of her fun,   45
And how she went a-hunting with dog and with gun.
" And now I have got him so fast in my snare,
I'll enjoy him forever, I vow and declare."

AUTHOR UNKNOWN

Barbara Allen

All in the merry month of May,
    When green buds they were swelling,
A young man on his death-bed lay
    For love of Barbara Allen.

He sent his servant to her then,   5
    To the place where she was dwelling.
" Oh, haste and come to my master dear,
    If you are Barbara Allen."

Slowly, slowly rose she up
    To the place where he was lying;   10
And when she drew the curtains up
    Says, " Young man, I think you're dying."

" Oh, it's sick I am, and very, very sick,
    And 'tis all for Barbara Allen."
" Oh, better for me you'll never be,   15
    Though your heart's blood were a-spilling."

" Oh, do you remember, young man," she says,
    " When the red wine you were filling,
That you made the healths go round and round,
    And slighted Barbara Allen? "   20

He turned his face unto the wall,
    And death with him was dealing:
" Adieu, adieu, my dear friends all;
    Be kind to Barbara Allen."

She had not gone a mile or two,   25
    When she heard the death-bell knelling;
And every toll the death-bell struck
    Cried, " Woe to Barbara Allen! "

" Oh mother, mother, make my bed,
    To lay me down in sorrow.   30
My love has died for me today,
    I'll die for him tomorrow."

AUTHOR UNKNOWN

Johnny Armstrong

This ballad is a story of treachery, but its main effect is one of heroism rather than horror. The Armstrongs were independent lords who lived on the border and refused to be allied either with the English or the Scots, and the death of their betrayed leader was proudly recorded in their annals.

There was a man in Westmoreland,
    John Armstrong was his name;
He had nor wealth nor noble blood,
    But widespread was his fame.

He kept eight score men within his hall,   5
    With steeds all milky white;
They had gold bands about their necks,
    And their weapons were all alike.

News had been brought unto the king
    That Johnny was living free,   10
As bold and daring a wild outlaw
    As roamed the northern countree.

The king he wrote a letter then,
　　A letter large and long;
He sent it to Johnny in his own hand   15
　　And promised to do him no wrong.

The morrow morning at ten of the clock
　　To Edinburgh went he,
And with him all his eight score men,
　　A goodly sight to see.   20

When Johnny came before the king
　　He fell down on his knee;
" Oh, pardon my sovereign liege," he said,
　　" Oh, pardon my men and me."

" Thou shalt not be pardoned, thou traitor knave,   25
　　Nor the eight score men with thee;
Tomorrow morning by ten of the clock
　　Thou shalt hang on the gallow-tree! "

Johnny took the bright sword from his side,
　　It was sharp and swift to play;   30
Had not the king stepped quickly aside
　　His head had been cut away.

" Fight on, my merry men," Johnny cried,
　　" And see that none are ta'en;
Rather than men should say you were hanged   35
　　Let them see how you were slain."

Then like a madman Johnny fought,
　　Like a mad army then fought he,
Until a false Scot came from behind
　　And ran him through his fair body.   40

" Fight on, my merry men," he cried;
" I am hurt, but I am not slain;
I will lay me down to bleed for a while.
Then I'll rise and fight again."

AUTHOR UNKNOWN

May Colvin

Although most of the old ballads are devoted to violence and sudden death, some of them are light-hearted. A few are even humorous. "May Colvin" is sometimes known as "The Western Tragedy," but, although the poem proceeds from romance to the threat of murder, the conclusion is anything but tragic.

False Sir John a-wooing came,
    To a maid of beauty rare;
May Colvin was the lady's name,
    Her father's only heir.

He wooed her indoors, he wooed her out,   5
    He wooed her night and day;
Until he got the lady's consent
    To mount and ride away.

" Go fetch me some of your father's gold
    And some of your mother's fee,   10
And I'll carry you to the far Northland
    And there I'll marry thee."

She's gone to her father's coffers,
    Where all his money lay;
And she's taken the red, and she's left the white,   15
    And lightly she's tripped away.

She's gone down to her father's stable,
　　Where all his steeds did stand;
And she's taken the best and left the worst,
　　That was in her father's land.   20

He rode on, and she rode on,
　　They rode a long summer's day,
Until they came to a broad river,
　　An arm of a lonesome sea.

"Leap off the steed," says false Sir John;   25
　　"Your bridal bed you see;
For it's seven fair maids I have drownèd here,
　　And the eighth one you shall be.

"Cast off, cast off your silks so fine,
　　And lay them on a stone,   30
For they are too fine and costly
　　To rot in the salt sea foam."

"O turn about, thou false Sir John,
　　And look to the leaf of the tree;
For it never became a gentleman   35
　　A naked woman to see."

He's turned himself straight round about
　　To look to the leaf of the tree;
She's twined her arms about his waist,
　　And thrown him into the sea.   40

"O hold a grip of me, May Colvin,
　　For fear that I should drown;
I'll take you home to your father's gates,
　　And safe I'll set you down."

" O safe enough I am, Sir John,   45
    And safer I will be;
For seven fair maids have you drowned here,
    The eighth shall not be me!

" O lie you there, thou false Sir John,
    O lie you there," said she,   50
" For you lie not in a colder bed
    Than the one you intended for me."

So she went on her father's steed,
    As swift as she could away;
And she came home to her father's gates   55
    At the breaking of the day.

Up then spake the pretty parrot:
    " May Colvin, where have you been?
What has become of false Sir John,
    That wooed you yestere'en? "   60

" O hold your tongue, my pretty parrot,
    Nor tell no tales on me;
Your cage will be made of the beaten gold
    With spokes of ivory."

Up then spake her father dear,   65
    In the chamber where he lay:

" What ails you, pretty parrot,
    That you prattle so long ere day? "

" There came a cat to my door, master,
    I thought 'twould have worried me;   70
And I was calling on May Colvin
    To take the cat from me."

                          AUTHOR UNKNOWN

Get Up and Bar the Door

Broadly humorous ballads have had a long history. Most of the comic song-stories center about the domestic scene, as in " Get Up and Bar the Door," where a homely little world is pictured with exact details: the wind blowing in through the cracks of the walls; the puddings simmering on the stove; the good housewife with her hand in her household work.

It fell about the Martinmas time,
    And a gay time it was then,
When our goodwife got puddings to make,
    And she's boiled them in the pan.

The wind so cold blew south and north,   5
    And blew across the floor;
Quoth our goodman to our goodwife,
    " Get up and bar the door."

" My hand is in my household work,
    Goodman, as ye may see;   10
And it will not be barred for a hundred years,
    If it's to be barred by me! "

They made a pact between them both,
  They made it firm and sure,
That whosoe'er should speak the first,   15
  Should rise and bar the door.

Then by there came two gentlemen,
  At twelve o'clock at night,
And they could see neither house nor hall,
  Nor coal nor candlelight.   20

" Now whether is this a rich man's house,
  Or whether is it a poor? "
But never a word would one of them speak,
  For barring of the door.

The guests they ate the white puddings,   25
    And then they ate the black;
Though much the goodwife thought to herself,
    Yet never a word she spake.

Then said one stranger to the other,
    " Here, man, take ye my knife;   30
Do ye take off the old man's beard,
    And I'll kiss the goodwife."

" There's no hot water to scrape it off,
    And what shall we do then? "
" Then why not use the pudding broth,   35
    That boils into the pan? "

O up then started our goodman,
    An angry man was he;
" Will ye kiss my wife before my eyes!
    And with pudding broth scald me! "   40

Then up and started our goodwife,
    Gave three skips on the floor:
" Goodman, you've spoken the foremost word.
    Get up and bar the door! "

AUTHOR UNKNOWN

The Turkish Lady

This is a storytelling song discovered in the Kentucky mountains by Tom Scott, the American ballad-singer. Like many ballads, it is based on a true story about a famous knight, Lord Batesman, and his adventures in the East.

There was a man, and he lived in England,
And he was of some high degree,
He become uneasy, ill-contented
Some far-off, foreign land to see.

He sailed to East, he sailed to West,   5
He sailed all over the Turkish shore,
Until he was caught and put in prison,
Never to be released any more.

Now the Turk he had but the one lone daughter,
The fairest these two eyes ever did see;   10
She stole the keys to her father's dwellin',
And resolved Lord Batesman she'd set free.

She drew him down to the deepest cellar,
She drew him a cup of the strongest wine;
She says, " Each hour would seem like a minute,   15
Oh, sweet Lord Batesman, effen you was mine."

They made a vow, they made a promise,
They made a vow, they made it stand;
He'd never wed no other woman;
She'd never wed no other man.   20

But seven long years done roll aroun',
It seem like they was twenty-nine.
She wrapped up her clothes in a great big bundle,
And resolved Lord Batesman she'd go find.

She went till she come to Lord Batesman's castle,   25
" And is his Lordship here within? "
" Oh yes, oh yes," cried the proud young porter,
" He's just now bringin' his new bride in."

The porter went to his master's chamber;
Down he went on bended knee,   30
"There is a lady at your gate, sir,
Fairer than your new bride ever can be.

"She has got rings on every finger,
And on one finger she has got three,
And enough gay gold around her middle   35
As would buy half Northumberlee.

"She bids you remember a piece of bread;
She bids you remember a cup of wine;
She bids you remember a Turkish lady
Who freed you from your close confine."   40

The lord he stamped on the chamber floor,
He broke that table in pieces three,
"Oh I'll foreswear all my lands and dwellin's
For the Turkish lady who set me free!"

AUTHOR UNKNOWN

Molly Malone

In Dublin's fair city where the girls are so pretty
There once lived a maiden named Molly Malone,
And she wheeled a wheelbarrow through streets wide and
    narrow,
Cryin', "Cockles and mussels, alive, alive, oh!"

She was a fishmonger, and faith! 'twas no wonder,
For her father and mother were fishmongers, too.

And they wheeled a wheelbarrow through streets wide and
    narrow,
Cryin', " Cockles and mussels, alive, alive, oh! "

And she died of a fever of which none could relieve her,
And that was the end of sweet Molly Malone.

Now her ghost wheels her barrow through streets wide and
    narrow,
Cryin', " Cockles and mussels, alive, alive, oh! "
" Alive, alive, oh! Alive, alive, oh! "
Cryin', " Cockles and mussels, alive, alive, oh! "

AUTHOR UNKNOWN

Shameful Death

This ballad by a nineteenth-century poet carries no date line, but the references to knights and the flowery names of the characters tell us that the action occurred in feudal times, in the Age of Chivalry. The speaker, a man of seventy, does not cry out at the outrage done to a younger man, a good friend and a fearless fighter. Nevertheless we sense his anguish and need for revenge that day when he saw the body of his friend swinging, with staring eyes, from the hornbeam tree where the cowards shamefully hanged him.

There were four of us about that bed;
　　The mass-priest knelt at the side,
I and his mother stood at the head,
　　Over his feet lay the bride;
We were quite sure that he was dead,　　　5
　　Though his eyes were open wide.

He did not die in the night,
　　He did not die in the day,
But in the morning twilight
　　His spirit passed away,　　　　　　　10
When neither sun nor moon was bright,
　　And the trees were merely gray.

He was not slain with the sword,
　　Knight's axe, or the knightly spear,
Yet spoke he never a word　　　　　　　15
　　After he came in here;
I cut away the cord
　　From the neck of my brother dear.

He did not strike one blow,
   For the recreants came behind,   20
In a place where the hornbeams grow,
   A path right hard to find,
For the hornbeam boughs swing so,
   That the twilight makes it blind.

They lighted a great torch then,   25
   When his arms were pinioned fast,
Sir John the knight of the Fen,
   Sir Guy of the Dolorous Blast,
With knights threescore and ten,
   Hung brave Lord Hugh at last.   30

I am threescore and ten,
   And my hair is all turned gray,
But I met Sir John of the Fen
   Long ago on a summer day,
And am glad to think of the moment when   35
   I took his life away.

I am threescore and ten,
   And my strength is mostly passed,
But long ago I and my men,
   When the sky was overcast,   40
And the smoke rolled over the reeds of the fen,
   Slew Guy of the Dolorous Blast.

And now, knights all of you,
   I pray you pray for Sir Hugh,
A good knight and a true,   45
   And for Alice, his wife, pray too.

                WILLIAM MORRIS

8
FOLK TALES
OF OUR TIMES

Casey Jones

Young in years though it is, America has already a mythology of its own. The heroes of its tall stories include giants like the mighty logger, Paul Bunyan, and hard-living, loud-laughing pioneers like Dan'l Boone and Davy Crockett. Since these folk characters lived free and reckless lives, it is natural that their songs are full of swing and bravado.

One of the most famous of American folk ballads is the one entitled "Casey Jones," the story of a brave engineer. He was a real person, born John Luther Jones. His town was Cayce (pronounced Casey) in Kentucky, and the incident actually happened. The date was April 30, 1900, and a tablet was subsequently erected to Jones's memory at Cayce. Part of it reads: "While running the Illinois Central Fast Mail, and by no fault of his, his engine bolted through three freight cars. Casey died with his hand clenched to the brake helve, and his was the only life lost."

> Come, all you rounders, if you want to hear
> The story 'bout a brave engineer;
> Casey Jones was the rounder's name,
> On a six-eight wheeler, boys, he won his fame.
>
> Caller called Casey at half-past four;   5
> He kissed his wife at the station door;
> Mounted to the cabin with orders in his hand;
> And he took his farewell trip to the Promised Land.

    Casey Jones, mounted to the cabin,
    Casey Jones, with his orders in his hand!   10
    Casey Jones, mounted to the cabin,
    Took his farewell trip to the Promised Land.

" Put in your water and shovel in your coal,
Put your head out the window, watch them drivers roll,
I'll run her till she leaves the rail,   15
'Cause we're eight hours late with the western mail! "

He looked at his watch and his watch was slow,
Looked at the water and the water was low,
Turned to his fireboy and then he said,
" We're goin' to reach 'Frisco, but we'll all be dead! "   20

Casey pulled up that Reno Hill,
Tooted for the crossing with an awful shrill,
The switchman knew by the engine's moans
That the man at the throttle was Casey Jones.

He pulled up within two miles of the place,   25
Number Four stared him right in the face,
Turned to his fireboy, said, " You'd better jump,
'Cause there's two locomotives that's a-goin' to bump! "

Casey said, just before he died,
" There's two more roads I'd like to ride."   30
Fireboy said, " What could they be? "
" The Southern Pacific and the Santa Fe."

    Casey Jones, mounted to the cabin,
    Casey Jones, with his orders in his hand!
    Casey Jones, mounted to the cabin,   35
    Took his farewell trip to the Promised Land.

T. LAWRENCE SEIBERT

How We Logged Katahdin Stream

The legend of Paul Bunyan is one of our mightiest myths, a symbol of pioneering America. Paul Bunyan is the gigantic woodsman, the great logger whose house was so tall that the top ten floors were hinged to let the moon go by. Singlehanded, Paul dug the Great Lakes; his falling axe made the Grand Canyon; he ran so fast that his shadow was always twenty feet behind him; his pet was a blue ox so huge that one hundred and seventy axe handles would equal the distance between her eyes. Paul's adventures have been related in many variations. One of the latest is a rhymed version which brings Paul to Maine, supposed to be the state of his birth.

Come all ye river-drivers, if a tale you wish to hear
The likes for strength and daring all the North Woods has no
    peer:
'Twas the summer of 1860 when we took a brave ox team
And a grand bully band of braggarts up to log Katahdin
    Stream.   4

Bold Gattigan was foreman, he's the pride of Bangor's Town,
And there was no other like Chauncey for to mow the great
    pines down;
Joe Murphraw was the swamper, with Canada Jacques
    Dupree.
We'd the best camp cook in the wilderness — I know, for it
    was me.

We left from Millinocket on such a misty day   9
We dulled our axes chopping the fog to clear ourselves a way,
Till at last we reached the bottom of Mount Katahdin's peaks
    supreme
And vowed that we within the week would clear Katahdin
    Stream.

O, Chauncey chopped and Murph he swamped and Canada
     Jacques did swear,
Bold Gattigan goaded the oxen on and shouted and tore his
     hair,
Till the wildwood rang with "*Timber!*" as the forest mon-
     archs fell,   15
And the air was split with echoes of our axe-blows and our yell.

For six whole days and twenty-three hours we threshed the
     forest clean —
The logs we skidded by hundreds, O, such a drive was never
     seen!
We worked clear round the mountain, and rejoiced to a jovial
     strain,
When what did we see but that forest of trees was a-growing
     in again!   20

Then all of a sudden the mountain heaved, and thunder spoke
     out of the earth!
"Who's walking around in my beard?" it cried, and it rum-
     bled as though in mirth.
The next we knew, a hand appeared — no larger than Moose-
     head Lake —
And it plucked us daintily one by one, while we with fear did
     quake!

Paul Bunyan held us in one hand! With the other he rubbed
     his chin.   25
"Well I'll be swamped! You fellers have logged my beard
     right down to the skin!"
"We thought you was Mount Katahdin," Gattigan shouted
     into his ear,
"We're sorry, but 'twouldn't have happened if the weather
     had been clear."

Well, good old Paul didn't mind it at all. He paid us for the
    shave —
A hundred dollars apiece to the men, to the oxen fodder he
    gave.   30
And now, ye young river-drivers, fill your glasses — fill mine
    too —
And we'll drink to the health of Bold Gattigan, and his gallant
    lumbering crew!

DANIEL G. HOFFMAN

The Cowboy's Lament

As I walked out in the streets of Laredo,
As I walked out in Laredo one day,
I spied a poor cowboy wrapped up in white linen,
Wrapped up in white linen as cold as the clay.

" Oh, beat the drum slowly and play the fife lowly,   5
Play the dead march as you carry me along;
Take me to the green valley, there lay the sod o'er me,
For I'm a young cowboy and I know I've done wrong.

" It was once in the saddle I used to go dashing,
It was once in the saddle I used to go gay;   10
First to the dram-house and then to the card-house;
Got shot in the breast and I'm dying today.

" Get six jolly cowboys to carry my coffin;
Get six pretty maidens to bear up my pall.
Put bunches of roses all over my coffin,   15
Put roses to deaden the sods as they fall.

" Then swing your rope slowly and rattle your spurs lowly,
And give a wild whoop as you carry me along;

And in the grave throw me and roll the sod o'er me
For I'm a young cowboy and I know I've done wrong."   20

We beat the drum slowly and played the fife lowly,
And bitterly wept as we bore him along;
For we all loved our comrade, so brave, young, and handsome,
We all loved our comrade although he'd done wrong.

AUTHOR   UNKNOWN

The Cowboy's Dream

Last night as I lay on the prairie,
   And looked at the stars in the sky,
I wondered if ever a cowboy
   Would ride to that sweet by-and-by.

They say there will be a great round-up,   5
   And cowboys, like cattle, will stand
To be marked by the Riders of Judgment
   Who are posted and know every brand.

I know there's many a stray cowboy
   Who'll be lost at the great final sale,   10
When he might have gone on to green pastures
   Had he known of the dim narrow trail.

They tell of another big Owner
   Who's ne'er overstocked, so they say,
But who always makes room for the sinner   15
   Who drifts from the straight narrow way.

They say he will never forget you,
    That he knows every action and look;
So for safety you'd better get branded,
    Have your name in his big Tally Book!

AUTHOR UNKNOWN

Jesse James

The name of Robin Hood has often been used in connection with Jesse James who, it was said, robbed banks and held up trains in order to help widows and orphans. There is little if any truth to this — James was a robber for gain and a desperado — but the ballad-makers kept up the legend for sentimental reasons. It was while James was in hiding that he assumed the name of Thomas Howard and was betrayed by Robert Ford, one of his own gang.

Jesse James was a lad who killed many a man.
He robbed the Glendale train.
He stole from the rich and he gave to the poor,
He'd a hand and a heart and a brain.

It was Robert Ford, that dirty little coward,   5
I wonder how bad he did behave;
For he ate of Jesse's bread and he slept in Jesse's bed,
Then he laid Jesse James in his grave.

Jesse was a man, a friend to the poor.
He'd never see a man suffer pain;   10
And with his brother Frank he robbed the Chicago bank,
And stopped the Glendale train.

It was on a Saturday night, Jesse was at home,
Talking to his family brave,
Robert Ford came along like a thief in the night,   15
And laid Jesse James in his grave.

The people held their breath when they heard of Jesse's death,
And wondered how he ever came to die;
It was one of the gang called little Robert Ford,
That shot Jesse James on the sly.   20

Jesse went to his rest with hand on his breast,
His killing was a disgrace;
He was born one day in the county of Shay,
And he came of a solitary race.

Jesse had a wife to mourn for his life,   25
Three children, they were brave;
But that dirty little coward that shot Mister Howard,
Has laid Jesse James in his grave.

                                              AUTHOR UNKNOWN

John Henry

The story of John Henry, the steel-driving folk hero, dates from the 1870's when the railroad men were driving the longest tunnel of that time through the mountains of West Virginia. Almost all the work was done by hand, and John Henry was the best of the workmen. He stood six feet two and his hammer weighed over twenty pounds. One day the boss bought a steam drill that was said to replace two men in work. John Henry claimed he could beat the steam drill by himself. It was man against machine.

John Henry was a little baby,
   Setting on his mammy's knee,
Said " The Big Bend Tunnel on the C. & O. Road
   Is gonna be the death of me,
      Lawd, gonna be the death of me."   5

One day his captain told him,
   How he had bet a man
That John Henry could beat his steam drill down,
   'Cause John Henry was the best in the land,
      John Henry was the best in the land.   10

John Henry kissed his hammer;
   White man turned on the steam;
Shaker held John Henry's steel;
   Was the biggest race the world had ever seen,
      Lawd, biggest race the world ever seen.   15

John Henry on the right side
   The steam drill on the left,
" Before I'll let your steam drill beat me down,
   I'll hammer my fool self to death,
      Hammer my fool self to death."   20

Captain heard a mighty rumbling,
    Said, " The mountain must be caving in."
John Henry said to the captain,
    " It's my hammer sucking de wind,
        My hammer sucking de wind."   25

John Henry said to his captain,
    " A man ain't nothin' but a man,
But before I'll let dat steam drill beat me down,

I'll die wid my hammer in my hand,
   Lawd, die wid my hammer in my hand."   30

John Henry hammering on the mountain,
   The whistle blew for half-past two,
The last words his captain heard him say,
   " I've done hammered my insides in two,
     Lawd, I've hammered my insides in two."   35

The hammer that John Henry swung
   It weighed over twenty pound;
He broke a rib in his left-hand side,
   And John Henry fell on the ground.
     Lawd, John Henry fell on the ground.   40

They took John Henry to the river,
   And buried him in the sand,
And every locomotive come a-roaring by,
   Says, "There lies that steel-drivin' man,
     Lawd, there lies that steel-drivin' man! "

AUTHOR UNKNOWN

The Big Rock Candy Mountain

" The Big Rock Candy Mountain " is the dream of a tired wanderer who imagined a lazy life where, without effort, he could have all the good things he desires. Other wanderers took up the song, and ballad singers varied it. It has become a kind of classic of humorous wishful thinking.

One summer's day in the month of May
  A weary man came hiking;
Down a shady lane near the sugar cane
  He was looking for his liking.
As he strolled along, he sang a song   5
  Of a land of milk and honey,
Where a man can stay for many a day
  And never think of money.

O, the buzzing of the bees and the cigarette trees,
  And the soda-water fountain,   10
Where the blue bird sings near the lemonade springs
  In the Big Rock Candy Mountain.

In that Big Rock Candy Mountain
  Police have wooden legs;
The bulldogs all have rubber teeth,   15
  And the hens lay soft-boiled eggs.
The trees let down their rich, ripe fruit
  And you sleep on silky hay.
The wind don't blow and there is no snow
  Forever and a day.   20

O, the buzzing of the bees and the cigarette trees,
  And the soda-water fountain,
Where the blue bird sings near the lemonade springs
  In the Big Rock Candy Mountain.

Apple pies grow on bushes below,   25
  And the crust is flaky and light;
Roast pigeons fly into your mouth
  And the skies are always bright.

There's a lake with stew and dumplings, too;
    Cakes to be had for the asking;   30
Time seems to fly 'neath a sugar sky
    As you spend your whole life basking.

O, the buzzing of the bees and the cigarette trees,
    And the soda-water fountain,
Where the blue bird sings near the lemonade springs   35
    In the Big Rock Candy Mountain.

                       AUTHOR UNKNOWN

The Bad-Tempered Wife

There are many stories in verse about henpecked husbands and sharp-tongued wives. They are found in all languages, in the Orient as well as in Europe. The following (recently popularized by Richard Dyer-Bennett, who is known as the twentieth-century minstrel) is an American variation of an old English ballad entitled "The Farmer's Curst Wife."

A farmer was plowing his field one day,
When the Devil came and to him did say,
"See here, my good man, I have come for your wife,
For she's the bane and torment of your life."

So the devil he h'isted her up on his back,   5
And down to hell with her he did pack;
But when they got there the gates they were shut,
With a sweep of her arm she laid open his nut.

There stood a small devil with ball and with chains,
She upped with her foot and she kicked out his brains;
Six little devils jumped over the wall,   11
Saying, "Take her back, daddy, she'll murder us all,"

So the devil he h'isted her up on his back,
And up to earth with her he did pack;
" See here, my good man, I have come with your wife,
For she's the bane and torment of my life."   16

The devil he said to the farmer then,
" You keep her; I don't want to see her again.
From the look on her face everybody can tell
She's not fit for heaven and she's too mean for hell."

AUTHOR UNKNOWN

Joshua Fit de Battle of Jericho

*American Negro singers from the first turned to the Bible for their
inspiration, for it seemed to be part of their own history. They un-
derstood the sufferings of the Israelites enslaved in Egypt, and rejoiced in their escape from their cruel taskmasters. In their spir-
ituals, Negroes sang often about Jordan and Jericho, with pointed
allusion to their own walls of slavery which were to come tumbling
down.*

Joshua fit de battle of Jericho,
    Jericho, Jericho,
Joshua fit de battle of Jericho,
    And de walls come tumbling down.

You may talk about your king of Gideon,   5
    You may talk about your man of Saul;
There's none like good old Joshua
    At de battle of Jericho.

Up to de walls of Jericho
    He marched with spear in hand.   10
" Go, blow dem ram horns," Joshua cried,
    " 'Cause de battle am in my hand."

Den de lamb-ram-sheep-horns begin to blow;
    Trumpets begin to sound.
Joshua commanded de children to shout —   15
    And de walls come tumbling down.

Joshua fit de battle of Jericho,
    Jericho, Jericho,
Joshua fit de battle of Jericho,
    And de walls come tumbling down.

NEGRO SPIRITUAL
Author Unknown

Casey at the Bat

It looked extremely rocky for the Mudville nine that day;
The score stood two to four, with but one inning left to play.
So, when Cooney died at second, and Burrows did the same,
A pallor wreathed the features of the patrons of the game.

A straggling few got up to go, leaving there the rest,   5
With that hope which springs eternal within the human
    breast.
For they thought: " If only Casey could get a whack at that,"
They'd put even money now, with Casey at the bat.

But Flynn preceded Casey, and likewise so did Blake,
And the former was a pudd'n, and the latter was a fake.   10
So on that stricken multitude a deathlike silence sat;
For there seemed but little chance of Casey's getting to the
    bat.

But Flynn let drive a single, to the wonderment of all.
And the much-despised Blakey " tore the cover off the ball."

And when the dust had lifted, and they saw what had occurred,
15
There was Blakey safe at second, and Flynn a-huggin' third.

Then from the gladdened multitude went up a joyous yell —
It rumbled in the mountaintops, it rattled in the dell;
It struck upon the hillside and rebounded on the flat;
For Casey, mighty Casey, was advancing to the bat.
20

There was ease in Casey's manner as he stepped into his place,
There was pride in Casey's bearing and a smile on Casey's
face;
And when responding to the cheers he lightly doffed his hat,
No stranger in the crowd could doubt 'twas Casey at the bat.

Ten thousand eyes were on him as he rubbed his hands with
dirt,
25
Five thousand tongues applauded when he wiped them on his
shirt;
Then when the writhing pitcher ground the ball into his hip,
Defiance glanced in Casey's eye, a sneer curled Casey's lip.

And now the leather-covered sphere came hurtling through
the air,
And Casey stood a-watching it in haughty grandeur there.
Close by the sturdy batsman the ball unheeded sped;   31
"That ain't my style," said Casey. "Strike one," the umpire
said.

From the benches, black with people, there went up a muffled
roar,
Like the beating of the storm waves on the stern and distant
shore.

"Kill him! kill the umpire!" shouted someone on the stand;
And it's likely they'd have killed him had not Casey raised his
  hand.   36

With a smile of Christian charity great Casey's visage shone;
He stilled the rising tumult, he made the game go on;
He signaled to the pitcher, and once more the spheroid flew;
But Casey still ignored it, and the umpire said, "Strike two."

"Fraud!" cried the maddened thousands, and the echo an-
  swered "Fraud!"   41
But one scornful look from Casey and the audience was awed;
They saw his face grow stern and cold, they saw his muscles
  strain,
And they knew that Casey wouldn't let the ball go by again.

The sneer is gone from Casey's lips, his teeth are clenched in
  hate,   45
He pounds with cruel vengeance his bat upon the plate;
And now the pitcher holds the ball, and now he lets it go,
And now the air is shattered by the force of Casey's blow.

Oh, somewhere in this favored land the sun is shining bright,
The band is playing somewhere, and somewhere hearts are
  light;   50
And somewhere men are laughing, and somewhere children
  shout,
But there is no joy in Mudville — mighty Casey has struck out.

ERNEST LAWRENCE THAYER

AUTHOR AND TITLE INDEX